DATE DUE			

William Henry Harrison, 9th president of the United States

William Henry Harrison

9th President of the United States

William Henry Harrison

9th President of the United States

Rebecca Stefoff

GARRETT EDUCATIONAL CORPORATION

Cover: *Official presidential portrait of William H. Harrison by James Reid Lambdin.* (Copyrighted by the White House Historical Association; photograph by the National Geographic Society.)

 Published by Garrett Educational Corporation, 130 East 13th Street, P.O. Box 1588, Ada, Oklahoma 74820.

Manufactured in the United States of America

Edited and produced by Synthegraphics Corporation

Library of Congress Cataloging in Publication Data

Stefoff, Rebecca, 1951-
William Henry Harrison, 9th president of the United States / Rebecca Stefoff.
p. cm.
Includes bibliographical references.
Summary: Presents the biography of the man, who, as a result of his actions in the Battle of Tippecanoe, Indiana Territory, eventually became the ninth President of the United States.
1. Harrison, William Henry, 1773–1841 – Juvenile literature. 2. Presidents – United States – Biography – Juvenile literature. [1. Harrison, William Henry, 1773–1841. 2. Presidents.] I. Title.
E702.S73 1990
973.5'8'092 – dc20
[B]
[92] 89-25652
ISBN 0-944483-54-2 CIP
AC

Contents

Chronology for William Henry Harrison

1773	Born on February 9 in Charles City County, Virginia
1787–1790	Attended Hampden-Sydney College in Virginia
1791	Enrolled in medical school at the University of Pennsylvania; joined the U.S. Army in October
1792–1795	Fought Indians in the Northwest Territory under General "Mad" Anthony Wayne
1795	Married Anna Symmes on November 25
1798–1799	Resigned from the army; became secretary of the Northwest Territory
1799–1800	Served as delegate from the Northwest Territory to the U.S. House of Representatives
1801–1812	Served as governor of the Indiana Territory
1811	Defeated the Shawnee Indians at the Battle of Tippecanoe on November 7
1812–1814	Served as a general in the War of 1812
1816–1829	Served in the U.S. House of Representatives, Ohio state senate, U.S. Senate, and as minister to Colombia
1836	Defeated for presidency by Martin Van Buren
1840	Elected President over Van Buren
1841	Took office on March 4; died in the White House on April 4

William Henry Harrison served as President for only a month before his death in office. He is remembered more as an Indian fighter and a frontier governor than as a national leader. (Library of Congress.)

Chapter 1

The Battle of Tippecanoe

Throughout the fall of 1811, a force of 910 men advanced slowly through the swamps, forests, and thickets of what is now western Indiana. At that time this region was called the Indiana Territory, and it was the northwestern frontier of the young United States. The men were officers and militiamen, or volunteer soldiers, from the Indiana Territory and from Kentucky.

On September 26 the group had left Vincennes, the capital of the territory, located on the banks of the Wabash River in the southern part of the Indiana Territory. Their goal lay several hundred miles north of Vincennes, where the small Tippecanoe River flowed into the larger Wabash. There the Shawnee Indians had established a settlement they called Prophet's Town, after one of their leaders, who was the prophet of a new Indian religion.

INDIAN RESISTANCE

Prophet's Town had become a rallying point for Indians of many tribes who were beginning to band together into a union, or confederacy, to resist the white settlers who were moving into their lands from the eastern states. The volunteer force from Vincennes was determined to crush this center of Indian resistance at Prophet's Town and thus make the territory safe for white settlers.

The leader of the white army was the governor of the Indiana Territory and an experienced Indian fighter. His name was William Henry Harrison—and he had been battling the Shawnee Prophet and the Prophet's brother, the warrior Tecumseh, on and off for nearly 20 years.

Expecting a Victory

As Harrison and his men hacked and marched their way toward Prophet's Town, the Indian warriors there grew quite confident, for they expected to win a major victory over the whites. Shabbona, an Indian assistant of Harrison's who was then living at Prophet's Town, reported that the braves expected Harrison to confront them from across the Wabash River. According to Shabbona, the Indians said among themselves, "If they stay on the other side, we will leave them alone, but if they cross the river, we will take their scalps."

The Indians knew that most of Harrison's men were volunteers, not real soldiers, and they said scornfully, "One half of them are calico peddlers. The other half can only shoot squirrels. . . . They will run when we make a noise in the night like wildcats fighting for their young."

But the Indians were dismayed to learn that Harrison had crossed the Wabash some distance south of Prophet's Town. As he approached, he did so along the *northwestern* bank of the river—the Indians' side. The Indians were unprepared for this tactic, and their surprise slowed them down. They were also slow in responding to the threat of Harrison's approach because Tecumseh, their war leader, was away from Prophet's Town, seeking new allies among other Indian tribes.

The Prophet, although he was a respected religious leader, was not a warrior—in fact, he had made a vow never to fight, and he did not take part in any battles. So this moment found the Indians sorely lacking in strong leadership. Harrison knew this quite well. He had chosen to attack Prophet's Town at this time precisely because he knew Tecumseh was away.

A Moment of Truce

By the afternoon of November 6, Harrison and his men had advanced to within a mile and a half of Prophet's Town. Scouting parties of whites and Indians, meeting on the trail, exchanged scowls and gestures of defiance, but no fighting actually broke out. Under a flag of truce, representatives of the two sides met on the open ground between the army and the town. They decided that Harrison's men should camp for the night, during which there would be no fighting, and that in the morning the leaders would hold a council in the hope of avoiding a battle. Harrison agreed to these terms.

The Indians also asked Harrison not to move his army any closer to town. They suggested a campsite: a large field on top of a steep hill just northwest of town, in the triangle formed by the junction of the Tippecanoe and the Wabash rivers. After sending two of his men, Major Marston Clarke and Major Waller Taylor, to inspect the campsite, Harrison accepted the Indians' suggestion and ordered his army to make camp for the night.

A Few Misgivings

Harrison had asked the Indians to provide a campsite with plenty of drinking water and firewood. The field to which they guided him had both of these things. He was less pleased, however, to see that it was surrounded on two sides by willow trees. He feared that these trees would offer cover to the Indians if they decided to creep up on the camp during the night.

In spite of his misgivings, Harrison had little choice but to set up camp. To attempt to move now would simply start an all-out battle just as darkness was falling. So his men fell out of their marching ranks, put up their tents, and lit their cookfires.

At the point of the triangle, overlooking the riverbanks, Harrison stationed a militia company of sharpshooters who were nicknamed the Yellowjackets for the short yellow coats they wore. Along the three sides of the camp, he mingled soldiers from his one regular army unit, the 4th Infantry, with the armed volunteers. Having fortified his position as best he could, Harrison withdrew into his own tent for the night. His pale-gray horse was tethered to a stake not far from his tent.

Sneak Attack

Late that night, a hundred or so Indians crept silently up to the camp. Shabbona reported that their plan was to sneak as close as possible to Harrison's tent, then burst out of hiding and kill the commander. He said that they had to "crawl half a mile on their bellies like snakes" in order to get into position in the center of the whites' camp.

At four in the morning, the 4th Infantry's bugle-blower, Adam Walker, stepped into Harrison's tent to ask if he should blow reveille—the bugle call that starts the army's day. Harrison sat up to pull on his boots, but before he could answer Walker's question, the predawn hush was shattered by the crack of a rifle shot, followed by a scream. Some sentry among Harrison's men, more alert than the others, had seen one of the crawling Indians and fired on him.

Shabbona later said that if that Indian had "lain still and died" quietly, the surprise attack might have been successful. Instead, however, the wounded brave cried out, and the other Indians answered with their own war cries, thus launching the attack ahead of schedule. Only a handful of the hundred Indians managed to reach the center of the camp—not enough to get to Harrison's tent or to do any real damage to the whites.

The Lucky General

Harrison's life was spared by fate that morning. Running from his tent, he looked for his horse, but it had slipped from its tether and wandered off. So Harrison jumped on a brown horse and rode among his confused men as they fumbled into their boots and scrambled for their muskets. Harrison's aide, Colonel Abraham Owen, found Harrison's horse and mounted it. An instant later, Owen was shot down by Indians lying in ambush—Indians who knew well that Harrison's horse was pale gray and who thought they had slain the leader of the whites.

Although the Indians had ruined their planned surprise attack by sounding the alarm too soon, they soon recovered and launched a series of fearless attacks against the whites. Legend says that one bullet from an Indian rifle knocked Harrison's hat off and another one grazed his skull, causing a trickle of blood to smear his features. Whether this tale is true or not, we do know that many of the Shawnee preferred to fight with their traditional weapons—bows and arrows—rather than with the white man's guns, although other braves did use guns that had been supplied by the British in Canada.

This 1846 illustration shows Harrison in a herioc pose, leading his forces into battle at Tippecanoe even though one of his lieutenants is trying to hold him back. Harrison's victory at Tippecanoe made him a hero to the Americans of the Old Northwest. (Library of Congress.)

A Bloody Combat

Once, twice, and three times the whooping Indians advanced against the lines of white soldiers. Each time they were beaten back. A junior officer named John Tipton assumed command of the Yellowjacket troops at the point after his two senior officers were killed. Tipton later described the battle as "a very bloody Combat" that lasted for "two hours and 20 minutes." He said that the sound of firing never stopped and that the Indians and white men were so mixed during the battle that "we could not tell the Indians and our men apart."

Finally, though, as Tipton reported, the battle came to an end. The Indians had fought fiercely. Indeed, they had been so brave that Shabbona, the Indian observer who was working for Harrison and the whites, said that he had never seen men show such great courage.

But in Tecumseh's absence, the Indians did not have a strong battle commander, for the Prophet did not fight. Rather, he stood on a hilltop, surrounded by Indian women and children, and chanted prayers for an Indian victory. Lacking a leader and a plan, the attackers fought as determined individuals, while the whites fought as an organized unit with a battle plan and a commander. The white man's method proved to be the stronger on this occasion, and the Indians were defeated. An hour or so after daylight, the surviving Indians fled the field of battle.

After the Battle

Of Harrison's men, 61 were killed and 127 wounded. Harrison ordered the dead men to be wrapped in American flags and buried in a single large grave, over which a fire was kindled in the hope of making the spot unrecognizable to wild animals or to the Indians.

It is not known how many Indians were killed or wounded. Tipton wrote that the Indians lost more men than the whites, but other accounts said that only 25 to 40 Indians were killed. Because the Indians carried off as many of their dead and wounded as they could, Harrison could not make an accurate guess at their numbers.

Following the battle, Harrison had his men build a log palisade, or wall, on top of the hill where they were camped.

They rested there for a day or so, tending their wounded and regaining their strength. Then Harrison led his army into Prophet's Town. They found the Indian settlement deserted except for one old man who had a broken leg. Harrison found a stockpile of British muskets, some of them still wrapped in canvas, that the Indians had chosen not to use. He and his men seized the guns (and also a few brass kettles and other trinkets that the men wanted for souvenirs), and then they burned down the houses in the town. They also set fire to the food stores and cornfields so that the Indians would not find anything to eat if they returned to the spot. Then Harrison triumphantly marched his troops back to Vincennes, hoping to reach home before the heavy snows of midwinter set in.

The Indians who had been driven away from Prophet's Town returned before long, with the Prophet among them. Their first act was to dig up the grave of the white soldiers and scalp the corpses. The scattered bones were reburied a year later by a United States general and his men who were passing through the area on military maneuvers. However, after Indians later dug them up once more, a party of settlers from the Indiana town of Terre Haute reburied the troubled remains in 1821. Then, in 1830 they were placed inside a large coffin engraved with the words, "Rest, Warriors, Rest."

CONFLICT OVER TIPPECANOE

The actual fighting at Tippecanoe lasted only for a few hours. But the wrangling and debates about the battle lasted for years. Some people felt that Harrison was a hero who had boldly defended the United States frontier against the menace of the red man and had opened up a huge tract of land for white use. Others felt that Harrison had gone beyond his legal authority in attacking Prophet's Town and that he simply used the glory of the battlefield to make himself famous and important.

It is certainly clear that Harrison did not hesitate to make his exploits known to the world. Almost before the dust of battle had settled, he wrote several proud reports of his success at Tippecanoe—one of these reports appeared in the *Spectator*, a New York City newspaper, at Christmastime. He also boasted in a letter to William Eustis, the nation's secretary of war in Washington, D.C., that "the Indians have never sustained so severe a defeat since their acquaintance with the white people."

An Act of War

But the truth is that Prophet's Town lay *outside* the treaty lands of the Indiana Territory. In other words, the settlement was located on land to which the United States government had no claim at all. In fact, the government had specifically confirmed the Indians' rights to that land. This meant that when Harrison led his soldiers against Prophet's Town, he was not defending American soil from the Indians. Rather, he was invading their own territory with his army. Such an action is recognized by all peoples and governments as an act of war. So it must be said that Harrison carried the war to the Indians.

Of course, Harrison felt that this hostile action was necessary in order to prevent the Indians from continuing to raid white territory. But not everyone shared Harrison's view. One who disagreed was President James Madison, who was displeased with Harrison for breaking the treaty. Harrison was well aware that he had acted without official permission and had gone against the President's wishes. A few months after the battle, he admitted to a friend, "I have indeed for some time expected to be called to Washington to answer for my invasion of the Indian country."

THE HERO OF TIPPECANOE

But the criticisms of Harrison soon blew over. He remained governor of the Indiana Territory, and no action was taken against him by Madison or anyone else. To most Americans of his time, Harrison truly *was* a hero, and they gave him the affectionate nickname "Old Tippecanoe," or just "Tip."

For a century and a half, the Battle of Tippecanoe was regarded as the heroic action of a dauntless Indian fighter who helped win the Old Northwest for his country. In recent years, however, more and more Americans have become aware that the whites' treatment of Native Americans was often far from heroic. In many cases, it was cruel, oppressive, and shabby.

Today, the relationship between Harrison and his foe, Tecumseh, is no longer seen as the simple drama of a noble white Indian fighter and a ferocious Indian. Instead, historians point out that both Harrison and Tecumseh—like all whites and Indians—had faults and virtues that should be recognized. But in his own lifetime, Harrison enjoyed great fame as the hero of Tippecanoe. And that brief battle on the banks of a small wilderness stream did more than just put Harrison's name in newspaper headlines throughout the states and the frontier territories. It eventually was to make him the ninth President of the United States.

Chapter 2

Child of the Revolution

Many years after the Battle of Tippecanoe, when William Henry Harrison ran for President, he was called "the log cabin candidate." His enemies and friends alike created an image of Harrison as a simple frontiersman, a common man of the American West. But although he won his nickname and his fame on the frontier, Harrison was not a country-born backwoodsman like Daniel Boone. He was born in surroundings as prosperous and civilized as any that the American colonies could offer—the plantations of Virginia. His ancestors on both sides of the family had been among the foremost leaders of the colonies for generations.

FAMILY HERITAGE

On his father's side of the family, William Henry was descended from five generations of Harrisons, all of whom were named Benjamin. The first Harrison in America had arrived in the colonies from somewhere in England—it is not known exactly where in England the family originated. By 1632, this Benjamin Harrison had settled in the Virginia colony, where he owned a large tract of land. He must have

Berkeley Plantation in Virginia, William Henry Harrison's birthplace, was built in 1726 on land purchased by his great-grandfather. (Library of Congress.)

been regarded as an important figure in the early affairs of the colony because he served as the clerk, or secretary, of the Virginia Council, a group of landowners who helped the governor administer the colony's business. This type of public and political service became a family tradition.

The son of the first American Harrison was another Benjamin Harrison. This man, Benjamin Harrison II, was the great-great-grandfather of the future President. Like his father, he was a prominent landowner who was active in the government of the Virginia colony. He served in the House of Burgesses, the colony's elected legislature, several times between 1680 and 1698. From 1698 to 1712, he was a member of the Virginia Council, as his father had been. This Harrison ancestor was also one of the founders of the College of William and Mary in Williamsburg, Virginia—an institution which is still considered one of the nation's finest colleges today.

Benjamin Harrison III, William Henry's great-grandfather, served as the attorney general of the Virginia colony from 1702 to 1705, the speaker of the House of Burgesses in 1705, and the treasurer of the colony from 1705 to 1710. It was this Harrison ancestor who bought from Governor Berkeley of Virginia a large tract of land on the James River that became the site of the Harrison family's plantation and mansion. The estate was called Berkeley, after the governor who had sold it to the Harrisons.

The fourth Benjamin Harrison was William Henry's grandfather. He farmed the plantation at Berkeley and helped to build the house, and he married a woman named Anne Carter, who was descended from King Henry III of England (1207–1272). Benjamin Harrison IV also followed the Harrison tradition of public service. He was a colonel in the militia, as the volunteer defense force of the colony was called, and he also served as the sheriff of Charles City County. During the decade between 1734 and 1744, he was several times a member of the House of Burgesses. He died suddenly years before William Henry's birth, struck and killed by lightning.

Discontent in the Colonies

The most famous of William Henry's ancestors was his father, Benjamin Harrison V. He was born at Berkeley, probably in 1726, and attended William and Mary College. After completing his studies, Harrison continued the family tradition of involvement in colonial politics by serving in the Virginia House of Burgesses for nearly three decades, from 1748 to 1774.

These were years of excitement and difficulty in the American colonies. Discontent with British rule over the colonies was growing rapidly, and the colonists began to take sides. Some remained loyal to King George III of England, but a growing number spoke up in favor of greater freedom for the colonies. This movement eventually led to the Declaration of Independence, the American Revolution, and the founding of the independent United States of America.

Benjamin Harrison V was one of the colonial leaders who disagreed with the way England ruled the American colonies, and he did not hesitate to criticize the British. When the English Parliament passed the Stamp Act of 1765, which required the colonists to pay a tax to have an official stamp placed on such documents as wills, contracts, land titles, and even newspapers, Harrison was one of many colonists who argued fiercely against what they believed to be unfair taxation. During the following decade, as relations between the colonists and England grew worse, Harrison's speeches in the chamber of the House of Burgesses continued to support the idea of fair treatment for the colonies.

"The Signer"

When the break finally came between the colonies and England, Benjamin Harrison V helped shape American democracy and was present at the birth of the United States. He served in the First and Second Continental Congresses. The Harrison family loved to tell the story of how, when the modest John Hancock was reluctant to accept the position as speaker of the Congress, Benjamin Harrison V simply picked Hancock up and carried him to the speaker's chair, while delegates from all 13 colonies roared with laughter.

On a more serious note, Harrison was the chairman of the committee that debated the question of whether or not to accept the Declaration of Independence that had been written by Thomas Jefferson, a fellow Virginian. The Declaration was accepted, of course, and Harrison was one of 56 men – seven of them from Virginia – who signed that historic document under these stirring words: "And for the support of this Declaration, with a firm reliance on the protection of Divine Providence, we mutually pledge to each other our Lives, our Fortunes, and our sacred Honor."

The Harrison family was deeply proud that one of its members had signed the Declaration of Independence, and a framed copy of the document was kept on the wall of the study at Berkeley. For several generations afterward, everyone in the Harrison clan called Benjamin Harrison V "the Signer."

The Signer's political career did not end with that famous signature. During the American Revolution, he was made the official correspondent in charge of sending messages and information from the Continental Congress to General George Washington on the battlefield. He left the national Congress when he was elected a member of Virginia's new legislature, the House of Delegates, where he was speaker from 1778 to 1781. He was governor of Virginia from 1781 to 1784, and then returned to the state legislature, where he served until his death.

The Signer's Family

Benjamin Harrison V married Elizabeth Bassett in 1748. Like the Harrisons, the Bassetts were a Virginia plantation family of English descent. They had arrived in the colonies around the year 1660. Several generations of Bassett men had been soldiers and public servants of the colony, much like the Harrisons. Elizabeth had been born in 1730 on the Bassett plantation, which was called Eltham and was located in New Kent County, Virginia.

The Signer and his bride had seven children: Elizabeth, born in 1751; Anna, born in 1753; Benjamin VI, born in 1755; Lucy (the year of her birth is unknown); Carter Bassett (birth year also unknown); Sarah, born in 1770; and William Henry, born in 1773.

Most of these Harrison children grew up to play some part in the history of the United States. Elizabeth's husband directed a hospital in Richmond during the American Revolution. Anna married a well-known Virginia judge named David Coupland. Benjamin Harrison VI was a paymaster general in the Revolutionary Army. Lucy's first husband, Peyton Randolph, was a junior officer in the service of the famous French soldier, the Marquis de Lafayette, who fought on the American side during the Revolution. Carter Bassett Harrison was a member of the Virginia House of Delegates from 1784 to 1786 and again from 1805 to 1808; he was a member of the United States House of Representatives from 1793 to 1799. But of all the Signer's children, it was the youngest, William Henry, who had the greatest part in shaping his country's future.

BIRTH AND CHILDHOOD

William Henry Harrison was born on February 9, 1773, at Berkeley. He was born near the end of the colonial period, just three years before his father signed the Declaration of Independence. This makes him the last American President to have been born before the Revolution—the last to have been born a British subject.

William Henry was a true child of the Revolution, growing up in a thrilling time of tumult, rumor, and war. He was only a year old when his father left for Philadelphia in 1774 to take up his duties in the Continental Congress. He was four years old when his father returned to Virginia to serve in the House of Delegates. During his childhood, William Henry met many of the men who would later be called "America's Founding Fathers," men such as George Washington, Benjamin Franklin, and Robert Morris, who visited Berkeley to talk politics with his father. It is likely that young William Henry overheard many anxious conferences about the progress of the war against the British Redcoats, as the soldiers in the British Army were called, and that he also listened to spirited discussions about what form of government and constitution the newly independent colonies should adopt.

The Attack on Berkeley

On one occasion, the American Revolution struck at the Harrison home. A unit of Hessians, German troops in the pay of the British Army, joined with some Virginians who remained loyal to England to attack the homes of leading Virginian revolutionaries. This unit was led by Brigadier General Benedict Arnold, a colonist who had transferred his loyalty to the British and who was despised by the revolutionaries as a traitor.

Under Arnold's command, the Redcoats seized and set fire to Richmond, the capital of Virginia, in 1781, when William Henry was eight. They then marched on Monticello, the home of Thomas Jefferson, who was forced to flee into the hills with his family. At the same time, Redcoats attacked Berkeley. The Harrisons had enough advance warning to escape, and all of the family were saved, but their slaves, horses, and furnishings were stolen and their livestock were slaughtered by the angry Hessians and loyalists. After this incident, the Harrison family lived for a while in Richmond while William Henry's father was governor.

Education of a President

Because William Henry was the youngest child in a large family, many of his brothers and sisters were nearly grown up when he was born. The only two who were near enough to him in age to be his playmates were his brother Carter and his sister Sarah, both of whom were the companions of his childhood.

All of the Harrison children were educated at home by tutors (private teachers) hired by their father. At the time William Henry began his schooling, the family tutor was a man named Ethan Randolph. Five days a week, Randolph gave instruction in Latin, Greek, arithmetic, literature, and history. Because Benjamin Harrison V believed that a good education was important, the young Harrisons sometimes had lessons on weekends, too: astronomy and geography on Saturdays and two hours of Bible reading on Sundays. The Harrisons were members of the Episcopalian Church, which was related to the Church of England. Many of the more well-to-do or aristocratic families in the colonies were Episcopalians.

William Henry did not distinguish himself as a pupil. In fact, his parents were sometimes disappointed that he was not a better student. "All during my youth," he wrote to a friend many years later, "my father admonished [scolded] me about my studies." William Henry also remembered that his father loved to talk about the family history, and that he took great pride in the patriotic and military accomplishments of the Harrisons. That pride was passed on to young William Henry.

Although Benjamin and Elizabeth Harrison may have been disappointed in their youngest son's schoolwork, they discovered with some surprise that he did excel in one area. That area was medicine. From his earliest youth, William Henry loved the idea of being a doctor, and he jumped at every chance to bandage the wounds—real and imagined—of the family, servants, and slaves. It is said that he even set the broken leg of a pet horse so well that when the horse doctor arrived, he had nothing to do but pat the 12-year-old William Henry on the head and murmur, "Well done."

Medical Studies

Being a doctor was considered a respectable career choice for a younger son such as William Henry. So, in the hope of encouraging his interest in medicine, William Henry's parents enrolled him in a course of premedical instruction at Hampden-Sydney College in Prince Edward County, Virginia, when he was 14 years old. In addition to medical subjects, William Henry's courses included more Greek and Latin, history, and geography. He also began the study of advanced mathematics and of rhetoric (the art of speaking and writing persuasively and well). He helped start a literary society at Hampden-Sydney and developed an interest in military history.

In 1790 William Henry's parents withdrew him from Hampden-Sydney because they felt that the school's religious instruction and practices were too strongly influenced by the

Methodist Church. At that time, Methodism was considered to be the church of the common people and often found itself at odds with Episcopalianism, although both groups belonged to the same large group of Christian churches known as Protestant.

After leaving Hampden-Sydney, William Henry studied a short time at another academy, this one located in Southampton, Virginia. He then spent the summer of 1790 in Richmond, living with his older brother Benjamin and serving as an apprentice (trainee) with a well-known surgeon named Dr. Andrew Leiper. The next step toward becoming a doctor was to attend a medical school, and the Harrisons decided to send William Henry to the University of Pennsylvania Medical School in Philadelphia. But when Benjamin and Elizabeth Harrison packed William Henry off to Philadelphia by stagecoach in the winter of 1790–1791, they did not realize that they were sending him to a far different future than the life of a doctor.

Chapter 3

From Scholar to Soldier

The Philadelphia to which Harrison traveled was the largest and wealthiest city in the young United States. It was also the nation's capital (and would remain so until 1800, when the seat of government was moved to Washington, D.C.).

As the center of political and economic life in the country, Philadelphia bustled with activity. Ships plied the waters of the broad Delaware River to dock at the city's piers; pedestrians and coaches crowded the cobblestone streets. And because Philadelphia was also a military headquarters, regiments of booted and uniformed soldiers drilled on large assembly grounds and marched through the city squares in weekly parades. Everything had an air of interest and importance that must have been very exciting to a young man who had never been so far from home before.

Just two years earlier, the United States had held the first presidential election under its newly adopted Constitution. To no one's surprise, General George Washington had been elected President. Now the hero of the American Revolution, often called "the father of his country," presided over the nation's government from offices in the center of the red-brick city, near the spot where Benjamin Harrison V had signed the Declaration of Independence 15 years ago. But William

To young Harrison, Philadelphia must have seemed a busy and exciting place in 1791. It was the capital of the United States as well as a commercial and military center. (Library of Congress.)

Henry's destination lay on the opposite side of Philadelphia, several miles from the Delaware River, across a much smaller river called the Schuylkill. There stood the University of Pennsylvania, one of the nation's first institutions of higher learning.

A FATEFUL DECISION

The University of Pennsylvania was founded in 1740 as a charity school for orphans and poor children. In 1753 Benjamin Franklin persuaded other leading citizens of the Pennsylvania colony to turn the school into an academy, or private school for top-quality education. Franklin, one of the most intelligent and creative Americans of the colonial period, was the first director of the academy and guided its destiny for many years.

The academy became a college in 1765, when the first medical school in America was established there. By Harrison's time, the college was called the University of Pennsylvania, and its medical school—together with the Pennsylvania Hospital, which stood downtown, close to the government buildings—was the center of the study of medicine in the United States. Harrison was enrolled here as a medical student. His instructor was Dr. Benjamin Rush, a scholar and patriot who was one of the prominent public men of the Revolutionary War era.

Under Rush's guidance, Harrison entered the university's medical program. From his earliest childhood, he had shown more interest in doctoring than in anything else, and his family and teachers had been certain that he would grow up to become a doctor. But Harrison was soon to surprise everyone.

Death of the Signer

The first event that occurred after Harrison took up his medical studies was an unhappy one. His father, the Signer, died suddenly on April 25, 1791. Harrison received this sad news in Philadelphia. At the same time, he also learned that he had a new guardian to take the place of his father in managing his money and generally serving as an advisor to the 18-year-old William Henry. That guardian was Robert Morris, a well-known Philadelphia banker who had been a friend of Harrison's father.

Benjamin Rush: Patriot and Physician

During his lifetime, William Henry Harrison met many of the people who have gone down in history as Founding Fathers—the leaders of the Revolution and the young republic. One such great man whose life touched Harrison's was Dr. Benjamin Rush, his medical teacher, who was one of the most colorful characters of early America.

Born to a Quaker family near Philadelphia in 1745, Rush graduated from college at 15, studied medicine in Philadelphia for six years, and then completed his medical education at the University of Edinburgh, in Scotland. He returned to the American colonies in the late 1760s, just in time to be caught up in the struggle for independence.

Although he was busy as a doctor at the Pennsylvania Hospital and a teacher at the University of Pennsylvania, he found time to travel, write, and speak on behalf of the patriots' cause. He served in the Continental Congress and, like Harrison's father and his guardian, Rush signed the Declaration of Independence. He also served for a time as surgeon general of the Continental Army.

Rush was the friend of many prominent Americans, including Thomas Jefferson and John Adams. He was an earnest letterwriter, often corresponding with three or four friends in a day; some of his letters were many pages long. A number of the letters he wrote and received have been preserved, and they

Benjamin Rush was not only a doctor and a teacher but also a patriot who signed the Declaration of Independence. He was a lifelong friend of many of the nation's Founding Fathers, including John Adams and Thomas Jefferson. (Library of Congress.)

give historians a lively and rare look at the people, events, and daily life of Rush's day.

Rush wrote dozens of pamphlets and articles on social issues, and as a social thinker he was considered very advanced for his time. Among other things, he strongly believed that slavery should be abolished, that women should be allowed to attend college, and that alcohol should be banned. He also wrote many medical papers and books. His account of the yellow fever epidemic that struck Philadelphia in 1793 is still prized for its vivid description of the disease and its effect on the city.

In 1797, six years after Harrison left medical school, President John Adams appointed Rush treasurer of the national mint, which was located in Philadelphia. Rush held that post until his death in 1813.

Morris, like Harrison's father, was one of the signers of the Declaration of Independence. His greatest contribution to the future of the new country was his handling of the finances of the Revolutionary War. He obtained loans from the French and also gave of his own funds to buy weapons, ammunition, and food for the Continental Army. It is quite possible that without Morris' financial skills, the Revolution might have gone bankrupt before it succeeded in winning independence for the colonies. He was certainly a capable guardian for young William Henry Harrison.

At the same time that Harrison was mourning his father's

death and trying to keep up with his beginning courses in anatomy and medicine, history was in the making on the western frontier of the United States. Now that the war with England was over and the new Constitution and government of the United States were established, the American people turned their attention westward, where the frontier was seething with settlers, conflict, and excitement.

The Old Northwest

Under the Articles of Confederation, which served as the nation's first constitution until the Constitution of 1787 was officially adopted, a huge region lying to the west of the original 13 states was identified as the Northwest Territory. This territory was the first public land of the new country—that is, land that belonged to the government instead of to individual owners. It consisted of all the lands that lay west of Pennsylvania, east of the Mississippi River, north of the Ohio River, and south of the Great Lakes. The present-day states of Ohio, Indiana, Illinois, Michigan, and Wisconsin, as well as part of Minnesota, cover what was once the Northwest Territory.

Although the word "Northwest" is used today to mean the Pacific Coast states of Washington and Oregon, in Harrison's time it meant the Northwest Territory, which was the frontier, or edge of settlement and civilization. For this reason, the Northwest Territory is sometimes called the Old Northwest.

Much of the Northwest Territory had been claimed by the British or French before the Revolution. Although the United States had held claim to the region since the Treaty of Paris in 1783 (the treaty that officially ended the Revolutionary War), many of the British and French settlers and traders who had entered the territory from Canada were very reluctant to see it pass out of their control.

Indian Attacks

The biggest obstacle to American control of the Northwest Territory, however, came from the Indian inhabitants of the region. Some of the tribes living in the territory were far from eager to see white soldiers and farmers advancing into lands that the Indians considered to be their own. During the late 1780s, the Indians attacked some white settlements along the Ohio River, sometimes massacring and scalping the whites, sometimes kidnapping them and holding them prisoner.

As more and more settlers and their families pushed west to the wide-open spaces of the Northwest Territory, the Indian attacks increased, and a military force under General Josiah Harmar was crushingly defeated by Indian warriors. President Washington viewed the Indians on the frontier as an urgent danger to America, and he decided to increase the number of U.S. Army soldiers stationed along the Ohio and north of the river in the territory.

Sometime in the summer of 1791, Washington issued a call for emergency volunteers to fight in the Indian wars. That call was repeated on large bulletins that were posted throughout the country over the President's signature. Many such posters were placed on trees and walls around Philadelphia, where they attracted knots of curious and eager readers.

Military Ambitions

Perhaps one of these bulletins fired the patriotic enthusiasm of William Henry Harrison, the young medical student. Perhaps Harrison had been thinking about his family's tradition of public service through military and political activity, and wondering how he could carry on that tradition. Or perhaps he simply realized that he was not cut out to be a doctor after all. Whatever his reason, he made an important decision in October of 1791, just after his second year of medical school had started. He wrote to both his mother and to Robert Morris, his guardian, saying that he wanted to leave school and join the army.

Opposition to Plans

Neither Morris nor Elizabeth Harrison liked the idea. Harrison's mother felt that he should continue in the course that had been planned for him, finishing medical school and then becoming a doctor. In addition, she more than likely dreaded the thought of her youngest child going off hundreds of miles to a wild and unknown frontier to fight Indians.

Morris shared Elizabeth Harrison's opinion that the Indian wars were too rough-and-tumble for a young Virginia gentleman—especially William Henry, who was not particularly strong or hardy. (A full-length portrait of Harrison painted at about this time shows that he was slender and of average height, with brown hair and a thin face. Only his firm chin and the serious expression of his deep-set eyes give a hint of the stubborn, determined character he would display throughout his adult life.)

In spite of the opposition of those around him, Harrison persisted, refusing to give up the idea of soldiering. He informed his mother and his guardian that he had already written to President Washington's secretary of war, General Knox, offering his services. He had even written to the President himself, asking for an appointment with the nation's leader so that he could request an officer's commission.

In the face of such determination, Morris and Harrison's mother gave in. They told Harrison that if the War Department accepted his services, he had their permission to enlist. All that remained for him was to meet "the father of his country" face to face. He learned that the President had granted him an appointment.

MEETING THE PRESIDENT

Harrison was both excited and nervous as he prepared for his meeting with President Washington. "I rose early that October morning. I dressed carefully in my very best apparel," he remembered much later in his life. The fine clothes he donned with such care probably looked very much like the clothes he wears in his portrait: a velvet jacket with long lace cuffs, knee-length breeches, and square-toed boots with silver buckles.

Many years afterward, Harrison wrote a letter to a friend, describing his emotions upon being shown into Washington's office. "How I wished, at that moment, my father were alive to go with me," he said. "I was fearful that President Washington would consider me a nuisance, only another pestiferous son of a distinguished father who wanted a favor. Looking backward on that momentous day I wonder whence I summoned the boldness to present myself." He added that he stood straight and stiff, "to keep my knees from knocking" with nervousness as Washington crossed the room to shake his hand.

The President spoke briefly of his long-ago visits to Berkeley, Harrison's childhood home, and even remembered that he had once held the child William Henry on his knee. He also expressed his sympathy and sorrow at the death of Harrison's father.

It is clear that the conversation that followed made a great impression on Harrison and made him a lifelong admirer of Washington. Harrison recalled, "The President talked with me at considerable length about my plans for the future, about his own youth in Virginia, the rigors of military life, the pressing problems of the new Northwest Territory—all before touching on the matter for which I had come." He added that Washington appeared "much older and graver [more serious] than I had remembered. Yet his dignity, force, and general bearing were most impressive. I resolved in my heart to model my own life, as best I could, after his."

Ensign Harrison

President Washington was sufficiently impressed with the nervous but determined young man who stood before him that he offered to make Harrison an ensign, or junior officer, in the First Infantry Regiment, which was then stationed in Philadelphia. The President instructed the secretary of war to prepare a commission (certificate of officership) for Harrison, and he signed it that very day. By sunset, William Henry Harrison was an officer in the U.S. Army.

As an ensign, Harrison held a rank above that of the ordinary enlisted soldiers but below all the other officer ranks. The position would give him the opportunity to prove himself to his superiors; if he did well, he would be promoted. That night, he may have dreamed of winning glorious promotions by victories on the battlefields of the frontier. Such victories would indeed eventually come Harrison's way.

But Harrison's first military duties were considerably less exciting. He was made a recruiting officer. This meant that he was in charge of signing up new soldiers to fight in the Indian battles; their pay was $2 a month, and his was not much more. At the same time, he had his own training to attend. He had to learn military etiquette and commands: how to address senior officers, how to march, and how to do everything the army way.

Off to the Frontier

At that time, the training of a new ensign usually lasted about three months. Harrision was both surprised and excited, therefore, when he received his first active-duty orders only four weeks later. His commanding officer instructed him to take a company of 80 recruits (the new soldiers whom he had recently signed up) and march them to Fort Pitt. From there, he was told, he would be sent on to Fort Washington.

Fort Pitt was located at the site of present-day Pittsburgh, near the western border of Pennsylvania. And Fort Washington, located on the Ohio River where Cincinnati now stands, was well inside the Northwest Territory. Just one month after becoming an army officer, Harrison was on his way to the wild frontier.

Chapter 4

Into the Northwest Territory

Harrison's first task as an officer was to get his company of 80 raw recruits from Philadelphia to Fort Pitt. It was a journey of 250 miles, during which the men would have to pass through many types of terrain. The trip would be a real test of leadership for the young ensign.

The day after receiving their orders, Harrison and his company, accompanied by 10 mule-drawn wagons filled with supplies, headed west from Philadelphia on the Lancaster Road. The regimental drummer marched them out to a brisk rhythm, and the men wore their new uniforms proudly. They covered 20 miles that first day.

BY ROAD AND RIVER

For some distance beyond Lancaster, the rolling hills of the countryside were dotted with the neat, well-tended farms of Dutch and Quaker farmers. Gray stone houses clustered at every crossroad, and the road was wide and smooth.

But Pennsylvania, although it had been one of the original colonies and was the site of the national capital, was far from thickly settled. Once beyond the fertile farmlands of Lancaster, the men found that the houses grew smaller and fewer. The road, too, was less well-maintained; it became narrow and rutted. Thick forests overshadowed the road, littering its muddy surface with the red and gold leaves of autumn.

As the days passed, the men's uniforms became stained and dusty. Their eager pace slowed as the road wound through the rugged Allegheny Mountains—some days they were lucky to cover 12 miles. Frequently, the supply wagons would become bogged down in the mud or ruts of the trail. The men would then have to stop their march, unload the wagons, and haul them out. Special care was taken to guard the supplies, because the wagons carried not only food but precious gunpowder for the defenders of the western forts.

The company made camp each day at sunset. Often a few men ventured into the forest in search of squirrel, deer, or wild turkey to supplement their army rations, which consisted of salted pork, tea, and hominy (a kind of corn porridge) with molasses. As soon as the sun rose the next morning, the men were on their feet and marching again.

As they rounded a turn in the trail one day, Ensign Harrison and his men caught sight of the American flag waving in the breeze above a log building in the distance. The flag was the Stars and Stripes; red and white stripes, with a circle of 13 white stars on a blue background in the upper left corner. The log building was Fort Pitt. Twenty-one days after leaving Philadelphia, they had reached their first goal.

Fort Pitt

Like all forts on the frontier, Fort Pitt was a sturdy square stockade made of logs roughly hewn from the trees of the surrounding forest. A tower rose at each corner of the wall for gunners and lookouts. Inside the stockade were barracks, stables, and storehouses.

Later in his life, Harrison admitted that he had not known what to think of the soldiers at Fort Pitt. He was a young officer, filled with visions of glory and military splendor, and he believed it was important to keep his boots shined, his uniform neat, and his salutes sharp.

The men of Fort Pitt, however, were not very much like the smartly uniformed regiments Harrison had seen on parade in Philadelphia. Indeed, they more closely resembled backwoodsmen like Daniel Boone. Few of them wore regulation army hats. Some wore homemade hats of fox fur or raccoon skin, often with the tails hanging down in back; others went bareheaded. Even some of the officers had adopted this informal style.

As far as uniforms were concerned, the majority of the men dressed like Indians, in sturdy rawhide trousers and long shirts of deerskin. Instead of army boots, they wore Indian-style moccasins. In addition to rifles and muskets, many of the soldiers carried long hunting knives thrust through their belts, and some carried tomahawks, as the Indian fighting axes were called. In short, these tough frontiersmen were unlike any soldiers that young Ensign Harrison had ever seen.

Learning a Lesson

Harrison learned an important lesson about these rough-looking soldiers on his fourth day at Fort Pitt. He happened to be walking past a stump outside the fort when he noticed a gray-haired soldier sitting there, oiling a musket. Harrison was annoyed that the man did not salute him—in fact, the fellow did not even appear to notice that an officer was present. Harrison then noticed that the man's musket was old and battered, with a bent barrel. Speaking rather sharply, he asked, "How can you hit anything with that old bent musket?"

After taking a long look at the impatient young officer, the old soldier got to his feet and pointed to a wooden peg sticking out of the gate of the fort, about 30 yards away—certainly not an easy shot. The man then raised his gun and, without even seeming to take aim, fired a single shot. Harrison ran to the gate. To his astonishment, he saw that the musket ball had driven the peg into the wood. From that moment, he was less critical of the unsoldierly appearance of the frontier fighters, knowing that their lack of polish did not mean that they were not good soldiers.

Training in Frontier Combat

Harrison found himself thrown together with three young lieutenants who were also on duty at Fort Pitt. Their names were John Whistler, Meriwether Lewis, and William Clark. Along with these three, Harrison received some special training from experienced veterans in frontier combat.

They learned how to use knives and tomahawks—and they learned that this often became necessary in wilderness fighting, when the gunpowder ran out or the muskets jammed. They learned how to fight the Indians by using the Indian warriors' own techniques, such as scattering a regiment through the forest, hiding in trees to fire down at enemies on the ground, and marching in single file so that Indian trackers would not be able to guess their numbers by counting their footprints. They were taught how to notch blazes (knife slashes) into trees to mark a trail, how to pick campsites and avoid ambushes, and how to ford streams and lay roads across swamps.

This crash course in wilderness combat techniques was designed to prepare inexperienced officers for field duty in a short time, and it worked. Before long, Harrison was able to hit a target with a thrown tomahawk and to slip through the woods as quietly as an Indian.

New Friends

Lewis and Clark became Harrison's particular friends. In the short time he spent with them at Fort Pitt, he developed respect for their courage and spirit. None of them knew it at the time, but Lewis and Clark were destined to become even more famous than Harrison. In a few years, they would set forth on an epic journey of discovery and adventure in the vast unknown lands beyond the Northwest Territory. They would cross the Great Plains and the Rocky Mountains, reach the Pacific Ocean, and return to tell the waiting world about the wonders of the American West.

Long before that time, however, Harrison made another journey of his own. After only a month or so at Fort Pitt, he was told that it was time for him to carry out the second part of his original orders: to take his regiment down the Ohio River to Fort Washington.

ON THE OHIO

Pittsburgh stands today on the spot where two rivers, the Allegheny and the Monongahela, flow together to form a third, larger, river—the Ohio. This was the site of Fort Pitt, and the Ohio River was the natural highway for all traffic that moved westward from the fort. Floating downstream on flatboats was easier and quicker than hacking a path through the forested hills. So Harrison and his company found to their relief that the trip to Fort Washington would be much pleasanter than the hike to Fort Pitt had been.

The men took passage on several of the large flatboats that were carrying settlers and freight into Ohio. The settler families were bringing everything they owned with them. Their cows, chickens, dogs, and horses rode on the decks of the flatboats, and bales and crates of household goods, farm tools, and provisions were lashed down everywhere. Barrels of molasses, gunpowder, nails, sugar, and other goods, bound for St. Louis or for destinations as far away as New Orleans by way of the Mississippi River, also occupied much of the space on the crowded vessels.

Once all the passengers and cargo were aboard, the rivermen took up their positions along the decks of the boats, poles in hand. These hardworking men would guide the flatboats downstream all the way to Fort Washington, pushing against the river bottom with their poles to steer the boats or to speed them when the river grew sluggish. When the boatmen cast off the ropes that moored the boats to the Pennsylvania bank at Fort Pitt and pushed out into midstream, William Henry Harrison knew that he had entered the Northwest Territory at last.

Fort Washington

As the flatboats approached the riverbank at Fort Washington a few days later, Harrison was dismayed to see soldiers running or walking around in front of the fort without any guns. Some soldiers were even lying on the ground, as if ill or too tired to move. As soon as his boat landed, Harrison leaped ashore, to be greeted with the grim news that Indians had recently attacked the fort, killing half the men, taking

Fort Washington was built in 1790, just a few years before Harrison arrived there with his troops. It guarded the gateway to the Northwest Territory and later became part of the city of Cincinnati. (Library of Congress.)

many scalps, and wounding the commanding officer, General Arthur St. Clair. Here was real frontier warfare. Everyone expected the Indians to return at any moment to finish off the fort.

Harrison and his men set to work repairing the fort's defenses, distributing the supplies they had brought, and getting the wives and children of the settlers in the surrounding area moved inside the stockade. Throughout the winter, the garrison at Fort Washington waited tensely for a renewed attack, but not a single Indian approached the fort.

In the meantime, however, messages had reached President Washington, telling him of the attack on Fort Washington. The President immediately asked for more volunteers to increase the frontier forces. He also asked a retired general, one of the heroes of the Revolution, to return to active duty as commander of the military forces in the Northwest Territory. That general was Anthony Wayne. He was to have a powerful affect on the career of young Ensign Harrison.

UNDER "MAD" ANTHONY'S COMMAND

Anthony Wayne, one of the most colorful characters in American military history, was born in Pennsylvania on New Year's Day in 1745. When he reached adulthood, he inherited his father's property and continued the family business, which was a tannery (a factory where leather is manufactured from hides). He seemed to be headed toward a comfortable future as a gentleman farmer and leather merchant—until the Revolutionary War broke out, and patriots throughout the colonies were called upon to take up arms.

Although he had no previous military experience, Wayne,

at 31 years of age, was given a colonel's commission. He was involved in fighting near the Canadian border, and he commanded Fort Ticonderoga in upstate New York, in an area hotly fought for by American and British forces. Wayne did so well that he was promoted to the rank of brigadier general early in 1777.

After taking part in the battles of Brandywine and Germantown in the Philadelphia area, Wayne then suffered a crushing defeat at Paoli, not far from Philadelphia, where his troops were cut down by British bayonets in a night attack. He spent the following winter with General Washington at Valley Forge, where he shared the cold and misery of the beleaguered Continental Army.

Acquiring a Nickname

Wayne was one of Washington's commanders in the Battle of Monmouth, New Jersey, in June of 1778, in which the two sides suffered about equal losses. But Wayne's greatest and most daring moment in the war came on July 16, 1779, when he led a band of foot soldiers in a bold charge against a 700-man British garrison at Stony Point, New York. Against all odds, Wayne succeeded in capturing the garrison, but some people claimed that the attack had been reckless and foolhardy. One soldier who deserted from Wayne's regiment rather than make the charge attempted to explain his desertion by saying that Wayne was "mad"– in the sense of being crazy or insane, not of being angry. Major General "Mad" Anthony Wayne's nickname dated from that occasion.

Wayne ended the war in Georgia, where, in 1790, the Georgia legislature elected him to the newly formed U.S. House of Representatives. After almost two years in the

House, however, he lost his seat there because of a dispute over frauds in the state elections. At that disappointing moment, when it appeared that Wayne's public career might be over, President Washington made him commander-in-chief of the U.S. Army and sent him west to fight the Indians.

Back to Fort Pitt

Wayne arrived at Fort Pitt in the spring of 1792 and made it his first headquarters on the frontier. A large number of new recruits from the eastern states also arrived at the same time, and all of them had to be trained. Harrison was among the officers who were called to Fort Pitt from other duty posts to help with this training. Now he was passing on to others the wilderness and combat lore he had acquired just a few months before.

Harrison must have performed his duties well. After a few months, Wayne promoted him to the rank of lieutenant. And in 1793, Wayne made Harrison one of his aides-de-camp (a commanding officer's assistant who stays close to the commander so that he can carry messages or do any other necessary services as quickly as possible).

Moving Forward

After about a year at Fort Pitt, during which new soldiers were added to the forces and training continued for all the men, Wayne decided that his troops were ready to move forward into the Northwest Territory. He announced that they would go to Fort Washington.

At this point, Lieutenant Harrison had to dip into the

money he had managed to save from his army pay and buy a horse for himself. The army did not provide horses for its lieutenants, but as an aide-de-camp to the commander, Harrison would need one. He found a settler who was returning to the East after an unsuccessful attempt at frontier life and bought the man's horse for $60. Harrison was pleased with his new stallion's energy and style. He named the horse Fearnaught, which means "afraid of nothing."

INDIAN TROUBLES

All during the time Harrison was at Fort Pitt and in the Northwest Territory, there was trouble with the Indians. The Indians resisted the white men's efforts to open up the territory to settlement, but the whites were just as determined to take possession of the land, a mile at a time if need be.

Although friendship, trade relations, and intermarriage between whites and Indians were not uncommon on the frontier, hostility and violence erupted often – and on both sides. To President Washington in Philadelphia and to Wayne and Harrison on the frontier, the Indian troubles seemed like sudden brushfires – no one could predict when or where they would next break out. Trouble flared up quickly and destructively, and then things would be quiet for weeks or months before fresh trouble arose somewhere else.

Different Beliefs about Ownership

In order to understand how the whites and Indians came to be so firmly opposed to each other in the Northwest Territory, it is necessary to know something about their different beliefs concerning the ownership of land. The whites were accustomed to think of land as being parceled out in well-defined lots to individual owners. They also shared the belief that the purpose of owning land was to *use* it, and that land that was not being used to grow crops or to house settlers was being wasted. If the whites obtained an Indian chief's mark on a land title in exchange for money or gifts, they felt that they had bought the land and were now its owners.

But the Indians did not really understand the notion of private land ownership. In their way of thinking about things, people were part of the natural world, just like trees and animals. Areas that were empty of human life or sparsely inhabited were not wasted; that was just the way they were, and the Indians did not think that they had to let white people settle there just because there was room for them. The land "belonged" to all the Indians who hunted on it or even walked through it occasionally, and therefore no single Indian, not even a chief, could really sell it to the whites.

When chiefs did sign the white men's deeds, treaties, or land titles, many other Indians regarded these transactions as meaningless and felt that they did not have to honor them. So most of the Indian trouble on the frontier boiled down to a simple question: Who owned the land? Both sides tried to answer the question by force.

Chapter 5

Wilderness Warrior

Upon his arrival at Fort Washington, General Wayne looked to the north, into the heart of the Indiana Territory. He knew that the Ottawa, Potawatomi, Miami, Shawnee, and Chippewa tribes who lived in that region—the present-day states of Ohio and Indiana—were gathering their strength to hold off the white soldiers and settlers. He also knew, or at least suspected, that the Indians were getting help in the form of guns and ammunition from the British in Canada, who would be more than pleased to see their former colonies lose control of the Northwest Territory. Even some of the American loyalists—those colonists who had remained loyal to England and opposed the Revolution—had fled into the frontier territory and were friendly with the Indians, hoping that the Indians would keep the United States from expanding westward.

To make matters worse, the U.S. Army's defenses in the region were not as strong as they should be. Only three small forts had been built north of Fort Washington. They were Fort Hamilton, Fort St. Clair, and Fort Jefferson. The line they formed stretched from Fort Washington about halfway to the Maumee River, near what is now the northern border of the state of Ohio. Wayne decided not to wait until the Indians descended upon these forts or upon Fort Washington for a second time. Instead, he would advance to meet them.

PUSHING NORTHWARD

In October of 1793, Wayne led a force of 3,630 men north from Fort Washington. They stopped briefly at Fort Hamilton, then moved on to Fort St. Clair. Near Fort St. Clair, one of the supply caravans was attacked by Indians; 15 men were killed.

As soon as Wayne arrived at Fort Jefferson, he announced that the column would continue to move forward, pressing into the forest. Two new forts would be built north of Fort Jefferson, near the present-day boundary between Ohio and Indiana. Wayne was pleased when his aide, Harrison, volunteered to lead a company to work on the forts.

Building New Forts

Throughout the winter and spring, Harrison was in charge of all the details of building the two new forts. Although he had no experience in building, he chose men from the regiment who had some skill in carpentry, or who had built log cabins, to form the company of workers.

It was a difficult task, made more difficult by the cold, wet weather of a Northwest Territory winter. First, the men had to clear the land where the forts would stand. Then they chopped oak and hickory trees, shaped them into logs by lopping off the branches and smoothing the sides, and hauled them through snow, mud, and thickets to the building sites. As they worked, they were constantly afraid that Indian arrows would come whizzing out of the woods to cut them down.

By May of 1794, however, the work was completed and the two forts were stocked with provisions and supplies sent up from Fort Washington. One of the new forts was called Fort Greenville; it stood on the spot where the city of Greenville, Ohio, stands today, about 80 miles north of Cincinnati. The other, located on the Indiana-Ohio boundary just east of present-day Portland, Indiana, was named Fort Recovery.

First Combat

Harrison received his first real taste of combat in June of 1794, about a month after the forts were completed. A group of Indians burst out of the woods and attacked a detachment of soldiers and a supply train a quarter of a mile from Fort Recovery. Harrison was one of several officers who led hastily dressed armed parties of soldiers out to help their comrades.

The attackers killed 22 soldiers and wounded 30 before the whites could get safely into the fort. But the Indian arrows did not do much damage to the stockade, and after three days the attackers retreated north into the trackless forests beyond the fort. General Wayne then led a band of soldiers to follow them. When the troops reached the banks of the Maumee River, he had them construct yet another fort. It was named Fort Defiance, because by building it in the heart of Indian territory, Wayne was defying the Indians.

A SCOUTING MISSION

Although he had done a good job on Fort Greenville and Fort Recovery, Harrison was not responsible for the building of Fort Defiance. This time, General Wayne had another assignment for him.

Wayne wanted two parties of scouts to survey the area and gather news of Indian movements and activities. The scouting parties would also carry gifts for Indian chiefs they met, in the hope that they could win some allies among the local tribes. One scouting party was to go upriver, along the

Maumee toward Lake Erie; the other would go downstream toward Indiana, into the area where a wandering tribe called the Shawnee was believed to be camping.

A Captain DeButts was assigned to lead the first scouting party, and Lieutenant Harrison was put in charge of the second. An Indian scout named Walli, who was half white and half Indian but worked for the whites, was assigned to Harrison's party. His knowledge of the Indian languages and his tracking skills would prove very valuable to Harrison.

Finding Shawnee

According to Harrison's account of the scouting mission, written several months afterward, they left Fort Defiance at dawn and sighted their first Indian about eight hours later. It was a boy who was crouched on the riverbank, working on a birchbark canoe. When he caught sight of the approaching whites, he leaped to his feet and fled. Walli told Harrison that they must be near an Indian village or camp.

That evening, the scouting party approached a Shawnee camp—a circular cluster of huts made of pole frames covered with hides. They could see men moving around a campfire, and one tall man wearing a mask seemed to be chanting or shouting. While Harrison and the others lay hidden in the bushes, Walli entered the camp, pretending to be a hunting Indian seeking shelter for the night. He would learn what he could about the tribe's activities and return as soon as possible.

Walli was gone for an hour or so, and when he returned his expression was serious. He explained that the tall, masked man was the tribe's religious leader, and that he had been calling on the spirits to protect the Shawnee and drive off the white men. But, Walli added, Tecumseh, the Shawnee chief, was not at the camp. Apparently he was on a mission to see another Indian chief, perhaps Little Turtle, the leader of the nearby Miami Indians.

Harrison wondered what Tecumseh could be up to. He had heard tales of this stern, young war leader. Many frontiersmen regarded him as the most dangerous Indian in the Northwest Territory. Tecumseh and his brother, the tribe's religious leader, were to play an important role in Harrison's life for many years to come.

THE LEADER OF THE SHAWNEE

The details of Tecumseh's birth and early life are not fully known, but he was most likely born around 1768 in a Shawnee village called Piqua, which was located near where Springfield, Ohio, stands today. His name means "Shooting Star" in the Shawnee language. He had several brothers and sisters, including a brother about seven years younger who, as a child, was called Laulewasika, which means "Loud Mouth," for he was quite a talker. This brother would grow up to be the Shawnee Prophet.

A Hatred of Whites

It is said that Tecumseh's loathing of the whites stems from the murder of his father, a chieftain, by a band of white men when Tecumseh was a young boy. That hatred grew stronger in July of 1780, when a troop of white soldiers under the command of George Rogers Clark, a hero of the Revolution, attacked the village of Piqua and burned it to the ground, killing many of the tribe's warriors and forcing Tecumseh and his brothers and sisters to flee to the woods for their lives.

Shabbona, the half-Indian, half-white scout who knew both Tecumseh and Harrison well, said in later years that Tecumseh's hatred was "the most bitter of any Indian that I ever knew." And Tecumseh himself once said that he was unable to look upon a white man's face "without feeling the flesh crawl upon my bones."

Becoming a Shawnee Warrior

Tecumseh, the Shawnee chief who was Harrison's strongest opponent on the frontier, was raised by his older sister Tecumapease. His upbringing at Piqua followed the tribe's traditions.

Shawnee boys attended school, at which they were taught handcrafts (such as making canoes and weapons) as well as how to hunt and fight. They also learned Shawnee tribal history, which was not written in books but handed down from generation to generation in the form of songs, poems, and stories that everyone knew by memory. In addition, they learned all the rules of good conduct and etiquette that were part of Shawnee life. Two moral qualities that the Shawnee especially admired were honesty and respect for old people.

Sports were also part of the typical Shawnee childhood. Boys and girls alike played a game that was similar to modern American football. The playing field covered four or five acres and the teams numbered about 100 on a side. At the end of the game, the spectators gave rewards to the players who had played best, whether they were on the winning team or not.

Shawnee boys often engaged in mock battles, both for fun and to sharpen their fighting skills. They also liked to wrestle, and Tecumseh was considered an expert at this sport. He was so fond of it that he would wrestle anyone at any time. One white man who passed through Piqua when Tecumseh was a young man remembered seeing him wrestle in the snow.

When he was 16, Tecumseh passed a series of tests that all young men of the Shawnee had to face if they wanted to become warriors. To pass, he had to make his own bow and arrows and a war club, shave his hair (except for the long topknot worn by a warrior), hold hot stones in his hands without showing pain or fear, and live in the forest for one month without supplies or weapons, eating only what he could trap or catch with his bare hands.

But the most severe test was to kill an enemy and bring his scalp back to the village. Tecumseh did so, and he fastened the scalp to the outside of his hut. In the eyes of his tribe, he was no longer a boy, but a man.

A Vision of Indian Unity

As a young man, Tecumseh had gained a reputation for traveling far and wide, and for fierce fighting. On several occasions, he took part in raids on white settlers' flatboats on the Ohio River and is known to have taken some scalps in these and other attacks. He was one of the leaders in the attack on General St. Clair's forces near Fort Washington, in which half of the white soldiers were killed or wounded.

After the Shawnee war leader Cheeseekau was killed in an attack on the white settlement at Nashville, Tennessee, in 1792, one branch of the tribe chose Tecumseh for its new chief—in spite of the fact that he was younger than many of the braves. He had been one of the leaders in the attack on Fort Recovery just a few weeks before.

In addition to fighting, the young Tecumseh also ranged widely through the central United States on hunting and exploring trips. He went as far east as Virginia and New York State, south to West Virginia and Tennessee, and west to Indiana and Illinois. As the Indian leader journeyed among the different tribes of the region and saw the tide of white soldiers and settlers inching forward into the Northwest Territory, he began to see how the Indians could hold their ground.

Tecumseh believed that if all the different, fiercely independent tribes could somehow be persuaded to unite against the common enemy, they would be much more powerful and better organized than if each tribe simply went its own way—or, as was often the case, fought each other as well as the whites. He started to think that a confederacy, or union, of all the tribes might be able to fight the U.S. Army and win.

Pontiac's Conspiracy

Tecumseh was not the first Indian leader to have visions of an Indian confederacy. Pontiac, the great chief of the Ohio Ottawa Indians, had fought against the British when they were building forts in the Great Lakes region. He, too, had realized that the Indians had a better chance of succeeding in battle against the whites if they worked together.

In 1763–1764 Pontiac persuaded a number of tribes to join a plan that was called "the conspiracy of Pontiac." Under this plan, each tribe agreed to attack the nearest British fort on a set date. The conspiracy was fairly successful—eight forts were captured and many British soldiers were slain. But after a defeat at the hands of a British relief force, the Indian tribes withdrew from the conspiracy. Pontiac tried to reunite them, but he died in 1769, and the vision of a united Indian confederacy appeared to have died with him. Several decades later, however, Tecumseh had the same dream—to unite the tribes. He would spend years of his life trying to reach this goal.

LITTLE TURTLE OF THE MIAMI

After Walli rejoined Harrison and the scouting party, they crept silently away from the Shawnees and made a fireless camp several miles down the trail. The next day, Harrison decided that they should go to Little Turtle's camp to see what was happening there.

Harrison and his scouting party found the camp of Little Turtle near the source of the Maumee River. Harrison wrote that Little Turtle himself came out of his teepee to greet them, and that he sent his women away from the teepee when he sat down to talk with Harrison (this was a sign of respect among Indian warriors).

Little Turtle was nearly 50 years old at this time, but he was still a forceful leader and a vigorous fighter. Not long before, he had defeated a Kentucky militia led by a Colonel Hardin and had taken 150 white scalps. The Miami chief was a talkative host who urged Harrison to smoke and drink with him. He also took great pride in showing Harrison such goods as axes, copper kettles, muskets, and cloth that he had purchased from white traders—or perhaps had received as gifts from the British.

A Peace Conference

It is possible, although it is not known for certain, that Harrison met Tecumseh in Little Turtle's teepee on this occasion. Some accounts say that Tecumseh was present; other versions

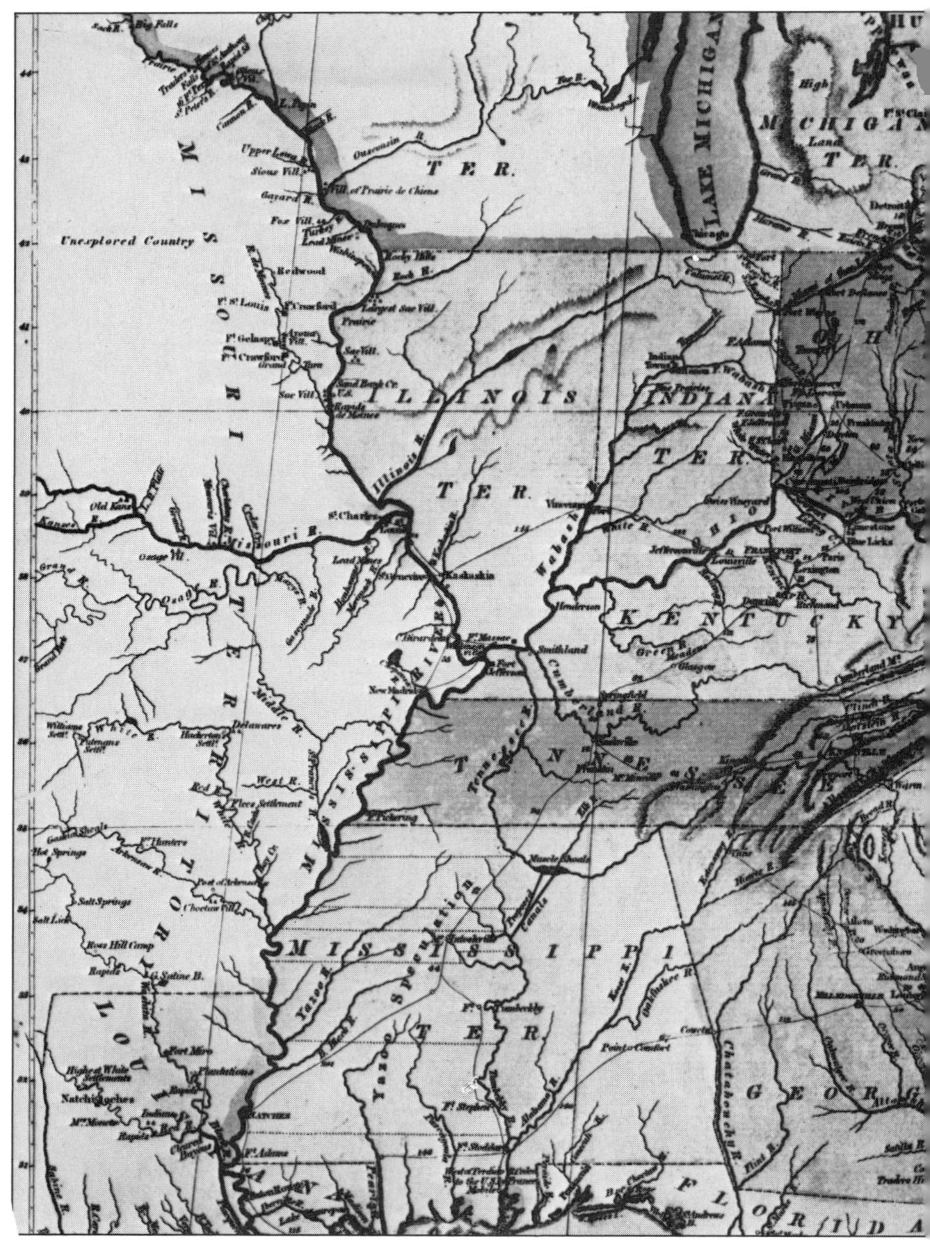

This map was made in the early 1800s, after Ohio achieved statehood and the Indiana and Illinois Territories were carved out of the Old Northwest Territory. It shows Vincennes and

Prophet's Town (here called Indian Town) on the Wabash River. (Library of Congress.)

of the story do not mention Tecumseh at all. Harrison's own account of the visit with Little Turtle is unclear on this question.

But Harrison and Little Turtle did discuss the problem of warfare on the frontier. Harrison urged the Miami chieftain to live side-by-side with the whites in peace and friendship, claiming that the land was big enough for both. Little Turtle answered that the land belonged to the Indians, and that he was afraid the whites would overrun it and outnumber the Indians. He may also have argued that because the Indians were hunters, not farmers, they needed a large expanse of unbroken forest to support the wildlife on which they lived.

This was another point of disagreement between whites and Indians. Whites felt that Indians would be happier, more prosperous, and generally better off if they settled down on farms—in other words, if they copied the white way of life. Some Indians were willing to do so, but many others preferred to continue their traditional wandering life, hunting and fishing over wide territories as their people had done for generations.

Harrison reported that he had tried to explain to Little Turtle that the whites did not want war, but that they now owned the lands. They would pay for the land they used, he said, but they *would* come. It would be better for all if the Indians greeted them in peace.

Little Turtle replied that he did not want war, either, but that he could not allow the whites to take over the Indians' land. At this point, it was clear that the two men could not agree and had nothing more to say to one another. Harrison made a polite farewell, gathered up his party, and left the Miami camp.

THE BATTLE OF FALLEN TIMBERS

Upon his return to Fort Defiance, Harrison reported to General Wayne that, although Little Turtle had treated him courteously, the Miami camp contained about a thousand warriors who appeared to be prepared for battle. He also told Wayne that the warriors at the Shawnee camp seemed to be working themselves up for a fight as well.

Once again, Wayne decided not to wait until he was attacked. He would take the battle to the Indians. Orders went out to all men to be ready to march at dawn. Wayne was going to attack Little Turtle's camp.

The Indians Unite

In the hot, humid weather of August 1794, Wayne's troops rode and marched along the muddy, forested banks of the Maumee. Along with them rode about 1,600 mounted soldiers from Kentucky who had been sent to increase Wayne's strength. His total fighting force was about 3,000 men.

Riding Fearnaught, Harrison stayed close to General Wayne in case the general had an order or a message to be relayed to one of his captains somewhere along the marching column. Like Wayne's other two aides, Harrison wore a green ribbon pinned diagonally across the front of his uniform so that everyone would recognize him and know that he spoke with the general's authority.

By August 20, Wayne had advanced to a point very near Fort Miami, an outpost of the British forces in Canada. But another force had also been moving toward the same spot. It was an army of between 1,000 and 1,500 Indians. Indian scouts had kept the local chieftains well informed of Wayne's movements from the moment he left Fort Defiance, and the chiefs had decided to meet his challenge. They combined their forces into a single army. Little Turtle brought Maumee warriors, Tecumseh brought Shawnee, Buckongahelas brought Delaware, Tarhe brought Wyandot, and Turkeyfoot brought Ottawa. The overall commander of the Indian army was Blue Jacket, a chief of the Shawnee.

Ambush

Wayne's advance was slowed when he ran into a roadblock–a pile of trees that had been blown down by a tornado. The trees not only blocked the trail but also created a high, thick barrier. Wayne cound not see beyond it.

Suddenly shots and arrows poured out of the fallen trees. It was an ambush! Blue Jacket's advance warriors had hidden among the trunks and branches of the trees and now were launching an attack. Loud war cries filled the air as fighting broke out up and down the trail and in the surrounding forest.

For at least an hour, the two forces continued to exchange fire. The disciplined rifle fire of Wayne's well-trained infantrymen held the Indians pinned down in their ambush–they could scarcely raise their heads above the logs. Gradually, the soldiers spread out in a large semicircle and began to move forward toward the Indians. Wayne wanted to encircle them and then close in as if tightening a noose. As soon as his men were close enough, he gave the order to charge with bayonets raised. The men ran forward toward the Indians and engaged them in hand-to-hand combat with their bayonets attached to their guns.

The Indians Retreat

Although he did not fight, Harrison made heroic contributions to the battle. He criss-crossed the battleground on Fearnaught, carrying Wayne's orders to the captains and bringing reports back to Wayne. It is said that a tomahawk thrown by an Indian grazed his ear and buried itself in a tree just behind him, and that he had to slash repeatedly with his sword at Indian warriors who tried to drag him from the saddle.

Tecumseh, meanwhile, was fighting fiercely on the other side. With a small band of followers – including Sauwaseekau, the only one of his older brothers who was still alive in 1794 – he took up a position in a dense thicket and held it for as long as he could. He refused to give up and move back until it became clear that the Indians were taking a terrible beating.

The battle did not go well for the Indians in general, or for Tecumseh in particular. His rifle jammed, and a moment later Sauwaseekau was killed at his side by an infantryman's bullet.

When he saw that the Indian forces had turned and were retreating through the woods as fast as they were able, Tecumseh led two or three other Shawnee on a final bold dash. They ran to a group of Americans who were guarding a horse-drawn cannon, drove off the soldiers with a flurry of quick blows, cut the leather harness that held the cannon in place, and galloped off on the stolen horses. Even in retreat, Tecumseh was never lacking in courage or style.

British Betrayal

At the time of the Battle of Fallen Timbers, the British and the Americans were not at war. Officially, peace had been agreed to by the Treaty of 1783. Therefore, the two sides could not attack each other directly on the frontier or anywhere else without starting an all-out war between the two countries. But the British worked against American interests indirectly.

For example, there can be no doubt that Blue Jacket's army had received help from the British garrison at Fort Miami. The British provided the Indians with guns and ammunition to use against Wayne's men. Some Americans believed that British Redcoats (soldiers) sometimes fought on the side of Indians while wearing Indian clothing and face paint. Harrison stated that white men with painted faces – either British soldiers or British subjects from the Detroit area – had taken part in the earlier attack on Fort Recovery. And about 70 British volunteer soldiers, led by a British officer named Captain William Caldwell, marched with Blue Jacket.

The British were understandably disappointed that the Indians had been defeated in the Battle of Fallen Timbers. But the Indians were even more bitterly disappointed by what the British did immediately after the battle. The outnumbered Indian army fled toward Fort Miami, hoping for help from the same British officers who had encouraged them to attack Wayne. But the British shut the gate of the stockade in their faces, locking them out.

In anger and despair, the Indians continued fleeing downriver on their own. Tecumseh, however, was one Indian who never forgot or forgave this betrayal by the British. Although later in his life he would fight with them as their ally, he never really trusted the British again.

A PERSONAL TRIUMPH

In the aftermath of the Battle of Fallen Timbers, it was learned that the American forces had lost 31 men; another 102 were wounded. The Indians, however, had lost nearly 500 – almost half of their fighting force, including many of their best warriors and most respected leaders. The Battle of Fallen Timbers was not only a crushing defeat for the frontier Indians, it put the U.S. Army in a strong position to control the Northwest Territory. It marked the end of an era of Indian wars in the territory and the beginning of a great upsurge in white settlement.

The battle also marked a personal triumph for William Henry Harrison. In a message written to President Washington on the day after the battle, General Wayne singled out his "faithful and gallant aides-de-camp" for their "essential service" in carrying his orders to all parts of the field and for their "bravery exciting the troops to press for victory." Harrison was mentioned by name. Perhaps, when Harrison learned of this honor, he remembered the office where he had met the President three years earlier and imagined Washington reading the message and thinking of the earnest young man whom he had made into an ensign. Harrison had come a long way since that October day in 1791.

Chapter 6

Frontier Statesman

Immediately after defeating Blue Jacket's army at the Battle of Fallen Timbers, General Wayne ordered his troops to scour the countryside for many miles around, burning the Indians' villages and destroying their cornfields. This was done so that any Indians who remained in the area or who returned there after fleeing from the battle would be so busy simply trying to survive the coming winter that they would not be able to make further war on the whites. Years later, Harrison was to do the same thing after his victory at Tippecanoe.

PUSHING ON

Wayne then returned to Fort Defiance. In September, however, he decided to take advantage of his victory to push his line of forts a little farther into the Northwest Territory. He advanced to the point where two small rivers, which today are called the St. Mary's and the St. Joseph, flow together to form the Maumee. There he built a fort that was named Fort Wayne. A city of the same name stands on that spot today, in the northeastern corner of Indiana.

Fort Wayne was completed by October 22, 1794, and soldiers and supplies were sent to it from the other forts. Wayne then withdrew down the line to Fort Greenville, which was about halfway between Fort Washington on the Ohio River and Fort Wayne. There he planned to spend the winter.

Preparing for a Treaty

The joining of several tribes under Blue Jacket's leadership had worried Wayne and other whites, who feared that it might be the beginning of the dreaded Indian confederacy. But after the Indians' defeat at the Battle of Fallen Timbers, the confederacy was no longer a threat. The alliance between the Ohio and Indiana chiefs broke down, and the warriors retreated into their separate tribal lands. They caused no trouble for Wayne throughout the winter.

Wayne was glad that the Indian troubles had died down, but he wanted to make sure that the frontier remained quiet for some time to come. Having broken the Indian alliance at Fallen Timbers, he decided to take advantage of his success and offer a treaty to the tribes. He sent out messengers in all directions, inviting all the chieftains of the area to Fort Greenville for a big peace conference that was to be held during the summer of 1795.

As one of Wayne's aides, Harrison would be expected to be on hand at the meeting. But in the spring of 1795, a month or so before the Indians were scheduled to arrive at Greenville, General Wayne granted some of his hardworking younger officers a three-week leave. Harrison left Greenville and headed south to enjoy a break from the demanding routine of life in a wilderness fort.

A SUDDEN ROMANCE

Harrison decided to spend his leave visiting some friends in Kentucky. Three weeks were not really enough to visit his family in the East. And perhaps he did not feel a particularly strong longing to return home, for his mother had died not long after he left the East Coast. He had received word of her death in 1792, while he was stationed at Fort Washington. So his ties to his family in Virginia had loosened somewhat, and his life was now centered in the frontier.

Historians do believe that Harrison had a short romance with a Philadelphia girl in 1794, however. It appears that he was in Philadelphia at some point during that year, perhaps on army business, and that he met and fell in love with a young woman who is known only as "Miss M."

In a letter to his brother Carter written in 1794, Harrison proclaims his love for "Miss M" and says that he hopes to marry her, although he fears that as a very junior army officer he will not be able to offer her much. Apparently the romance came to nothing, as there is no further mention of her in his papers.

ANNA SYMMES

But the three-week leave in the spring of 1795 changed Harrison's life forever. During it, he met the young woman who would become his wife, Anna Tuthill Symmes.

There are several versions of how Harrison and Anna met. One version says that they met in Lexington, Kentucky, while Anna was visiting relatives there. Another version says that they met in Fort Washington, which was close to her father's large new home at the settlement called North Bend (now part of Cincinnati). Some stories even say that Harrison was introduced to Anna by his old friend, Meriwether Lewis. But wherever he met her, there is no doubt that he fell quickly in love.

An Educated Young Woman

The girl who captured Harrison's heart was two years younger than he. She was born on July 25, 1775, in Morristown, New Jersey. Her mother was Susan Livingstone Symmes and her father was Judge John Cleves Symmes.

The Revolution broke out when Anna was less than a year old. New Jersey was the scene of many of the great battles of the war because British troops occupied much of the state. To get his daughter out of the combat zone, Anna's father disguised himself as a British soldier and carried the little girl through the enemy army on horseback, risking imprisonment – or maybe death – if he were discovered. He brought her safely to her grandparents' house on Long Island, New York.

Anna spent her entire girlhood on Long Island. There she received more education than most girls of her time. After attending a girls' school called Clinton Academy in Easthampton on Long Island, she went to a well-known private girls' school in New York City.

While Anna was growing up in New York, her father was serving as the chief justice of New Jersey's state supreme court. He managed to purchase a huge tract of land – half a million acres – in the Northwest Territory, along the Ohio River in what is now southern Ohio, and there he built an estate at North Bend. Anna came from New York to join him.

Courtship Problems

Little is known of the courtship of Harrison and his Anna. One thing that *is* clear from the records is that Judge Symmes did not approve of this young army officer as a suitor for his daughter. The judge was rich and influential; it is likely that he wanted her to marry someone more prosperous or established. He complained that Harrison could "neither bleed, nor plead, nor preach, and if he could plow I should be satisfied." The judge meant that Harrison was neither a doctor (a bleeder), nor a lawyer (a pleader), nor a preacher, and that the young man did not even have a farm to call his own.

The judge forbade his daughter to see Harrison. But apparently the two young people managed to spend some time together during Harrison's leave. At the end of his three weeks, however, Harrison had to return to Fort Greenville and his work there. General Wayne's great treaty meeting was about to get under way.

THE TREATY OF GREENVILLE

The 12 main tribes in the Northwest Territory sent representatives to the meeting at Fort Greenville. These were the Shawnee, Wyandot, Delaware, Ottawa, Chippewa, Potawatomi, Kickapoo, Kaskaskia, Wea, Piankeshaw, Eel River, and Miami Indians. In all, 92 chiefs and sub-chiefs attended. They brought many of their women and children and nearly a thousand warriors.

Wayne treated the Indians with smooth diplomacy. Instead of hurrying into discussions about the treaty he wanted them to sign, he let them set up a large camp and then hosted a feast that lasted for several weeks, with plenty of wild turkey and venison (deer meat) for his guests. He also provided them with plenty of rum, for the Indians had no alcoholic beverages of their own and many of them had grown extremely fond of the white man's liquor.

All of the food and liquor, as well as the gifts that Wayne exchanged with the chiefs, put the Indian leaders in a good mood. In addition, they knew after their experience at Fallen Timbers that Wayne had the stronger fighting force. So, when he finally suggested terms for a treaty, the Indian chiefs listened and then agreed.

Terms of the Treaty

The chiefs of the 12 tribes signed the Treaty of Greenville on August 10, 1795. The treaty established a line across the center of what is now the state of Ohio. This boundary, called the Greenville Treaty Line, divided the eastern part of the Northwest Territory between the whites and the Indians. The whites got southern and eastern Ohio and part of Indiana; the Indians agreed not to make war on the whites in this area. In addition, the Indians gave up 16 smaller, separate tracts of land, mostly around the frontier forts. All told, the United States gained treaty rights to about 25,000 square miles of the Northwest Territory under the Treaty of Greenville.

The Indians kept the lands north of the treaty line. The tribes were given trade goods—cloth, axes, liquor, and other supplies—worth about $20,000 for signing the treaty. They also were promised annuities, or yearly grants from the government, that would be worth a total of about $9,500 for all the tribes.

Blue Jacket signed the treaty for the Shawnee. Little Turtle, chief of the Miami, demonstrated his cleverness by passing off the Eel River Indians as a separate tribe. Wayne accepted this and gave them an equal share of the trade goods and annuities. In reality, however, the Eel River Indians were a part of the Miami tribe who happened to live west of Fort Wayne. Little Turtle was actually their tribal chief, too, so he received a double portion of payment from the whites: one share for the Miami and one for the Eel River.

A Dissatisfied Indian

One important name not found on the Treaty of Greenville is that of Tecumseh. He refused to attend the meeting because the defeat at Fallen Timbers had set him more firmly against the whites than ever before. He would not deal with them, and he scorned those chiefs who did.

Tecumseh declared that the chiefs who had signed the treaty had betrayed their people. He also warned that the treaty line would not hold back the whites, who would soon ask for more Indian land, and then still more. About half the Shawnee people agreed with Tecumseh. He led this group of followers to a new home near present-day Hagerstown, Indiana, west of the treaty line.

Tecumseh was disgusted with the Treaty of Greenville, but Wayne was delighted with it. From the President in Philadelphia to the humblest settlers along the Ohio, all the whites agreed that Wayne had put an end to the Indian wars. Now that he had succeeded in the mission Washington had given him, Wayne decided to retire. He and his staff returned to Fort Washington so that he could prepare to return to the East.

THE LOVERS ELOPE

Harrison was more than happy to go back to Fort Washington, of course, because it meant that he could see Anna. He visited North Bend as soon as he could get away from his duties. Anna was as glad to see him as he was to see her, and she agreed to marry him. There was just one big obstacle to be overcome, and that was Judge Symmes. Anna's father still did not believe that Harrison was a good enough match for his daughter. He ordered her not to see Harrison again.

Anna felt that it was no use waiting for her father to change his mind, for he might never do so. So, on November 25, 1795, she and Harrison took matters into their own hands and eloped. While Judge Symmes was in Cincinnati on business, Harrison and Anna fled to the house of Dr. Stephen Wood, the government-appointed treasurer of the Northwest Territory, who lived in North Bend. He was sympathetic to the young lovers and allowed them to be married in his home. Harrison was 22 years old; Anna was 20.

Because Harrison was still on duty at Fort Washington at the time of his marriage, the newlyweds had no honeymoon. Instead, they moved directly into the first of their many homes together, which was a small cabin just outside the fort.

An Angry Father-in Law

Judge Symmes was furious when he returned to Cincinnati and discovered that his daughter had run off to marry Harrison. He did not see his new son-in-law for two weeks after the wedding. They met at last, however, at a farewell dinner for General Wayne, who was ready to return to his home in the East.

The angry judge strode up to Harrison and demanded, "Just how do you propose to support my daughter?" Harrison replied, "By my sword, sir, and my good right arm."

Not impressed with Harrison's firm answer, Symmes continued to regret his daughter's marriage for some years. Only after Harrison became the well-known hero of Tippecanoe did the judge admit that his daughter had not made such a bad choice after all.

In spite of the judge's disapproval, though, the Harrisons appear to have had a happy and contented marriage. Anna Symmes Harrison never became a public figure. She was a quiet and private person, and little is known about her or the details of the Harrisons' marriage and family life.

A PROMOTION

Upon his departure, General Wayne turned command of Fort Washington over to Harrison, who was proud to have been chosen for this great responsibility. Wayne also sent a message to army headquarters in Philadelphia, recommending that Harrison be promoted to the rank of captain.

However, the promotion was not made official until May 15, 1797, just two months after President Washington left office and John Adams became the nation's second President, with Thomas Jefferson as his Vice-President. For a year and a half before that time, Harrison carried out all the responsibilities of a commanding officer. He was responsible for all army duties, including making sure that supplies and men were sent up the line to the other forts, as well as for maintaining order in the settlements.

Keeping order among the civilians was becoming a big

job, as swarms of new settlers arrived on every flatboat. Now that the Treaty of Greenville had ended the Indian menace, the Ohio River became an open highway to the treaty lands. Cincinnati, North Bend, and Fort Washington grew bigger and busier every day.

Harrison the Writer

At this point in his career, Harrison began a habit that would stay with him for the rest of his life. He started sending a great number of long, detailed reports to army headquarters, recounting everything that he did and all that was happening on the frontier.

In addition, Harrison worked hard to improve his writing style. He borrowed books from Judge Symmes and studied the works of ancient Roman writers such as the general Julius Caesar, the speechmaker Cicero, and the poet Horace. Drawing upon what he remembered from his rhetoric classes at Hampden-Sydney College, Harrison modeled his reports and letters on the works of these ancient masters.

Harrison spent long hours, late into the night, working with pen and paper. He bombarded army and government officials back East with hundreds of pages of letters and reports that were filled with information and suggestions about the Indians, the geography of the Northwest Territory, trade possibilities, and a host of other subjects. Perhaps it was because he showed himself to be so well informed on these issues that the government soon made a suggestion of its own. Captain Harrison received an offer from President Adams to make him the secretary of the Northwest Territory, at a salary of $1,200 a year.

TERRITORIAL OFFICIAL

Harrison resigned from the army in June of 1798 and took up the post of territorial secretary. The salary was welcome, as by now the Harrisons had two young children, Elizabeth and John. But he found the work of a territorial secretary rather boring; most of his duties involved filing land claims. Furthermore, he did not always see eye to eye with his superior, the governor of the territory, Arthur St. Clair. Governor St. Clair was a staunch member of the Federalist Party, the political party to which President Adams belonged, while Harrison favored the Republican Party, which was led by Thomas Jefferson.

By 1799 the Northwest Territory had enough settlers that it was allowed to send a delegate to the U.S. House of Representatives. The 21 members of the territorial legislature elected Harrison as the delegate. He won by one vote over Arthur St. Clair, Jr., the governor's son, who was then the attorney general of the territory. Harrison was now off to the nation's capital to represent the territory in the U.S. Congress.

But because the Northwest Territory was not a state, Harrison could not vote in the House of Representatives. However, he could suggest laws and enter into debates and discussions on issues that involved the frontier. Harrison served in the House from March of 1799 to May of 1800. His most significant achievement during that time was the Harrison Land Act, which helped determine how the western United States would be settled.

THE HARRISON LAND ACT

By the time Harrison entered the House, the country had grown by three new states: Vermont, Kentucky, and Tennessee. With the rapid rush of settlers to the Northwest Territory, it was clear that new states would be formed out of the territory very soon—and that settlement would expand into lands still farther west. But Harrison was disturbed that so much of the land on the frontier was being bought up by real estate companies or by wealthy landowners called speculators, not by the poor farming families who hoped to start a new life in the West.

Under the law at that time, land in the Northwest Territory could be sold in parcels of either 5,770 acres or 640 acres, and the lowest price possible was two dollars an acre. This meant that a man who wanted to purchase land for a farm had to have at least $1,280 in order to buy a 640-acre parcel—not to mention enough money for seeds, livestock, tools, and building supplies.

Harrison believed that the law should be changed so that families who did not have $1,280 for 640 acres could still buy a frontier farm. He introduced a bill that would allow territorial property to be sold in lots of 320 acres and that would permit buyers to pay for their property over a period of time after their farms were established.

Changing the American West

Many members of the House of Representatives found Harrison's proposal uninteresting—some of them even left the hall of Congress during his first two-hour speech on the subject. After all, the Northwest Territory was far away, and they had the interests of their own states to worry about. But Vice-President Jefferson and Representative Albert Gallatin of Pennsylvania agreed with Harrison and supported his proposal. They helped him persuade other congressmen of its importance. The Harrison Land Act was passed by the House and the Senate and became law in 1800.

Few people realized it at the time, but Harrison's bill

changed the destiny of the American West. It opened up the frontier to humble people of limited means. As much as anything else, the Harrison Land Act is responsible for the democratic, ruggedly individualistic character that was part of frontier and western life during the 19th century. It also earned Harrison high regard as a statesman in the Northwest Territory.

Chapter 7

Governor Harrison

The Northwest Territory was divided into two territories in 1800. The eastern portion, called the Ohio Territory, had the greatest number of settlers. Just three years later, in 1803, the Ohio Territory would have 60,000 inhabitants—enough to qualify for statehood.

The western portion of the Old Northwest was called the Indiana Territory. It was much larger than the Ohio Territory, covering part of northern Louisiana and all of the Northwest Territory except Ohio. This huge, wild tract needed a governor, and President Adams turned once again to William Henry Harrison, offering him the position.

In 1800 Harrison resigned from the House of Representatives to take up his duties as governor of the Indiana Territory. Starting on January 10, 1801, he would remain in that post for 11 busy, productive years.

INDIANA YEARS

The capital of the Indiana Territory was the small town of Vincennes, located on the east bank of the Wabash River, in what is today the southwestern corner of the state of Indiana. It had been founded nearly a century earlier by the French, who had built a fort on the site. The name "Vincennes" was in honor of the fort's first French commander. Vincennes was famous in Harrison's day as the scene of an important victory against the British forces by George Rogers Clark during the Revolutionary War.

Grouseland

Governor Harrison brought his wife and family to Vincennes in 1801. A third child, Lucy, had been born in 1800, and a fourth, William Henry, was born in 1802. Now that he had achieved an impressive position in the government, Harrison wanted to build a fine new home for his family. He obtained a large lot in the center of a walnut grove on the edge of town and designed a spacious brick mansion that was very much like the large plantation homes of his Virginia childhood. He sent East for building materials and furnishings.

The house, which Harrison named "Grouseland" for the swarms of game birds called grouse that lived in the walnut grove, took two years to complete. While it was being built, the Harrisons lived at the home of one of Harrison's friends in Vincennes, a wealthy trader named Colonel Francis Vigo, who was from the Mediterranean island of Sardinia.

The Harrisons moved into Grouseland in 1803. They lived comfortably there, with plenty of room for a growing family. Over the years, four more Harrison children would be born at Vincennes: John Scott, in 1804; Benjamin, in 1806; Mary, in 1809; and Carter, in 1811. Two more children were born to the Harrisons in Ohio, after they left Vincennes: Anna, in 1813, and James, in 1814. Of the couple's 10 children, only the youngest, James, failed to survive to adulthood. Harrison's was a remarkably healthy family at a time when many families lost as many as half their children to childhood diseases.

The Governor's Duties

Harrison chose one large room at Grouseland as his office, with a desk and bookshelves. When he had to hold large meetings with groups of settlers or Indians, he used the lawn as a conference place. He liked to entertain guests and held many parties and suppers at Grouseland for friends and members of the territorial government. Records show that in one year alone the Harrisons served 365 hams and 800 barrels of apple cider.

Harrison's duties as governor were quite varied. He was in charge of adopting laws, of appointing judges and military officers below the rank of general, and of commanding the militia (volunteer defense force). As the population of the territory increased, it was his job to divide it into townships and counties.

The area was rapidly becoming populated as the endless river of settlers flowed westward. When Harrison arrived in the Indiana Territory, the whole territory contained only two settlements other than Vincennes. By 1805, the territory had so many people that Harrison offered to resign so that a legislature could be elected by the settlers.

The following year, Harrison's old companions, Meriwether Lewis and William Clark, returned from their expedition beyond the Rocky Mountains with word of the vast unexplored plains that lay west of the Mississippi River. This meant that the Indiana Territory would now become the gateway to a new frontier, luring still more settlers into the area.

A Vote of Confidence

Despite Harrison's offer to resign, Thomas Jefferson, who had succeeded Adams as President, felt that Harrison's strong leadership was still needed and asked him to continue as governor. Later, James Madison, who succeeded Jefferson as President, made the same request.

The members of the territorial legislature sent a vote of confidence in Harrison to the new national capital in Washington, D.C. It read:

> We (the House of Representatives of the Indiana Territory) urge the reappointment of Governor Harrison:—because he possesses the good wishes and affections of a great majority of his fellow citizens; because we believe him to be sincerely attached to the Union, the prosperity of the United States, and the administration of its government; and because we have confidence in his virtues, talents, and republicanism.

Not everyone felt that Harrison was a good governor, however. Some people thought that he and other government officials who were from Virginia planned to create a way of life in the Indiana Territory like that of the South, complete with plantations and slaves. Slavery was banned in the Northwest Territory by the Northwest Ordinance of 1787, but Harrison's critics said—with truth—that he hoped to have that law changed.

Harrison, however, never did succeed in getting the Northwest Ordinance changed, and slavery remained forbidden in the territory. Meanwhile, Governor Harrison devoted some of his time and energy to development in Vincennes, helping to establish a junior college and a library there in 1806. But the most important of his duties involved Indian affairs.

The Treaty-Maker

In addition to being the territorial governor, Harrison was also the superintendent of Indian affairs for the Indiana Territory. In this role, he was responsible for making new treaties with the Indians whenever it was time to open up new lands to white settlement.

During his years at Vincennes, Harrison made a total of 13 separate treaties with various Indian tribes, obtaining rights to millions of acres of land in southern Indiana and Illinois. The first of these treaties was signed with the Wea, Kickapoo, and Delaware Indians in 1802. In 1804, Harrison and chieftains of the Sac and Fox tribes signed a treaty that gave the United States 15 million acres in Illinois and Wisconsin. In 1809, he made the Treaty of Fort Wayne with the Delaware, Miami, Eel River, and Potawatomi Indians. This treaty gave the United States three million acres in northern and western Indiana in return for annual gifts worth between $200 and $500 for each tribe.

One chief who did not sign any of Harrison's treaties was Tecumseh of the Shawnee. Throughout the early years of the 1800s, in fact, Harrison came to view Tecumseh and his younger brother as a growing problem.

TECUMSEH AND THE PROPHET

Tecumseh refused to deal with Harrison in any way and was angry at the chiefs who had signed the Treaty of Fort Wayne. He claimed that the treaty was illegal and threatened violence to any Indians or whites who attempted to enforce it. It appeared that the Indian wars were about to be renewed. And once again, the British in Canada were encouraging the Indians to fight the American settlers.

Tecumseh's old dream of an Indian confederation had not died after the Battle of Fallen Timbers. As the first decade of the century drew to a close, the dream was stronger than ever. Tecumseh continued to travel extensively, spreading his ideas about the Indian confederacy among dozens of tribes, all the way from the Canadian border to the Gulf of Mexico, as far east as New York and as far west as Minnesota. This time, the fiery Shawnee chief had religion on his side, with the help of his brother.

An Amazing Change

Tecumseh's younger brother, Laulewasika, had followed a very different path in life than that of Tecumseh. Unlike his older brother, Laulewasika was never much of a hunter or a fighter. Rather, he was known for his laziness and for his love of drinking. He made a habit of hanging around white forts and settlements in order to obtain alcohol. He was on hand at the signing of the Treaty of Greenville, and many people noticed his drunkenness there. After the treaty was signed, he remained in the Greenville area for some time, drinking rum whenever he could. In fact, for nearly a decade afterward, Laulewasika was an idle drunkard. Then an amazing change took place.

In early 1805, Laulewasika claimed to have had a series of religious visions, during which the Great Spirit—as the Indians sometimes called God—spoke to him in words of wisdom and inspiration. Almost overnight, Laulewasika's life changed. He stopped drinking and became a man of strict virtue, like Tecumseh. He also began to preach with great energy, urging the Shawnee to return to their ancient and honorable way of life and to uphold their traditional values.

With Tecumseh's help, Laulewasika founded a Shawnee settlement near Greenville. The two brothers attracted many followers. Some came because Laulewasika stirred their religious enthusiasm; others came because Tecumseh roused their pride and anger against the whites.

Tecumseh's brother, the Shawnee Prophet, helped unite the Indians against the whites by preaching a new religion. This portrait of the Prophet was painted by Henry Inman in the early 1830s. It was based on an earlier work by an artist named Charles Bird King. (The National Portrait Gallery, Smithsonian Institution.)

The New Prophet

In November of 1805, Tecumseh's brother proclaimed himself the new prophet, or religious leader, of the entire Shawnee nation—this is why he is often called the Prophet. He dropped the name Laulewasika and took a new name, Tenskwautawa, which means "the open door." He said that it was inspired by a verse in the Bible in which Jesus says, "I am the door." (It is clear that the Prophet knew something about the Christian faith. He is known to have spent some time with a group of Shakers, members of a small, enthusiastic Christian church that made some converts among the Indians.)

The Prophet's religious code was simple. It demanded just three things of the Indians: first, to drink no alcohol; second, to live in peace among themselves, with no fighting between the different tribes; and third, to give up the white man's ways and goods and return to the Indians' traditional ways. To this Tecumseh added a more military note: to resist the advance of the whites into Indian territory, by force if necessary. Believers flocked to their sides—Shawnee at first, then members of other tribes, in a trickle that quickly grew into a rushing flood.

The Prophet's Miracle

By April of 1806, Governor Harrison was convinced that the Prophet posed a serious threat to the security of white settlements on the frontier. In Harrison's view, anything that might help unite the Indians was dangerous, and the Prophet was bringing them together like never before.

To counter this threat, Harrison sent out a message to all the tribes, warning the Indians that the Prophet was a trickster. He said, "Demand some proof at least of his being the messenger of the Deity." Harrison said that the Indians should ask the Prophet to perform a miracle. He thought that this would be the Prophet's undoing. Little did he know how his suggestion would backfire.

The Prophet immediately answered the governor's challenge. He announced that on June 16 he would cause the sun to grow dark at midday. The Indians did not know it, but this was the date of an eclipse of the sun that had been predicted by white scientists.

How the Prophet learned of the coming eclipse is unknown. His spies may have found out about it from the college professors and government agents who were sent into the prairies to observe the event, or the British may have told him about it. At any rate, the Indians were greatly impressed when the Prophet "ordered" the sun to darken—and even more impressed when he "ordered" its light to return. News of this astonishing event spread from tribe to tribe like wildfire. To Harrison's dismay, the Prophet's power was greater than ever.

A Meeting at Grouseland

The Treaty of Fort Wayne in 1809 angered Tecumseh and the Prophet, who by then had moved their band of followers to Prophet's Town on the Tippecanoe River. Hearing of Tecumseh's rage, Harrison sent the chief a letter, urging him to honor the treaty. Harrison even offered to send Tecumseh to Washington, D.C., to speak to the President. Tecumseh, however, surprised Harrison by visiting the governor at his home in Vincennes.

In August of 1810, Tecumseh and the Prophet appeared on the lawn at Grouseland with 275 armed warriors. Telling his men to remain calm, Harrison had chairs placed on the lawn for himself and Tecumseh. Sitting in one, he offered the other to Tecumseh, who said with scorn, "The earth is my mother," and sat regally on the ground.

The Indians set up camp outside of town, and the governor and the chief made a number of formal speeches to each other over the succeeding days. Everyone was impressed with the speech-making skills of Tecumseh, who had acquired quite a reputation as a speaker. Unfortunately, only a few rough notes made by some of his listeners survive; none of his speeches were written down.

The meeting at Grouseland was dramatic, but it changed nothing between the whites and the Indians. Harrison repeated over and over that the whites meant the Indians no harm—they only wanted to use the land and would pay the Indians fairly for it. Tecumseh repeated over and over that no Indian had the right to sign a treaty or to sell tribal lands.

At one point, violence nearly broke out when the Shawnee chief leaped to his feet and accused Harrison of lying. Although the two men later spoke politely to one another, the conference ended on a threatening note. Tecumseh is said to have warned Harrison, "I want the present boundary line to last. If you cross it, I assure you the consequences will be bad." Then he and the Prophet and their followers left, heading back to Prophet's Town.

The Governor Takes Action

The meeting with Tecumseh at Grouseland made Harrison more certain than ever that big trouble was brewing with the Shawnee. He believed that Tecumseh was preparing to launch a new series of devastating Indian wars against the white settlements, and that only by attacking first could he save settlers' lives and avoid disaster. Thus it was that in November of 1811 Harrison led his famous attack on Prophet's Town and defeated Tecumseh's army in the Battle of Tippecanoe—the battle that won "Old Tip" his nickname.

The angry confrontation between Governor Harrison and Tecumseh at Grouseland in 1810 paved the way for the bloody Battle of Tippecanoe a year later. (Library of Congress.)

Their defeat at Tippecanoe at last put an end to the Indians' organized opposition to white settlement in the Northwest Territory. But Tecumseh was not involved in the battle. He would live to fight another day—and he and Harrison would soon meet on a new battlefield.

Chapter 8

War and Politics

After his victory at Tippecanoe, Harrison received votes of thanks from the legislatures of Kentucky and Indiana because the people there were so grateful to him for ending the threat of a Shawnee attack on their farms and towns. This gratitude would win many votes for Harrison a few years later, when he began running for political office.

TECUMSEH SEEKS REVENGE

No sooner had he returned to Vincennes from his successful campaign against Prophet's Town, however, than Harrison had to cope with new troubles on the northwest frontier. Tecumseh had returned to Prophet's Town to find his people scattered or killed and the town destroyed.

In a rage, Tecumseh blamed the Prophet for the Indians' defeat because he had left the Prophet in charge of the Shawnee while he went on his travels. It is said that Tecumseh even threatened to kill his brother. The Prophet was sent away to live in quiet disgrace with tribes to the west, and Tecumseh began to plan revenge against the whites for the attack at Tippecanoe.

Tecumseh knew that he could not defeat Harrison alone. He needed allies, and this time he looked to the British. Although he did not trust the British, Tecumseh knew that they wanted to cause as much trouble for the frontier Americans as they could, so they might provide guns and supplies for Indian warriors. Conflict was brewing between the British and the Americans – conflict that Tecumseh hoped to turn to the Indians' advantage. At the time of the Battle of Tippecanoe, in fact, England and the United States were on the verge of war.

THE WAR OF 1812

The roots of the War of 1812 between the British and the Americans lay in other wars on the European continent. Between 1793 and 1815, England was involved in a long series of wars with France. These were called the Napoleonic Wars, after French Emperor Napoleon Bonaparte. Thousands of British soldiers and sailors perished in this fighting.

The British navy, in particular, was in desperate need of manpower. So the British adopted the practice of kidnapping American sailors on the high seas and in foreign ports and forcing them to serve in the British navy. This was called "impressment," and it outraged the United States.

In addition, England interfered with U.S. trade with other countries – by blocking American ships from entering French ports to sell goods there, for example. There was also the continuing unrest along the border between the United States and Canada, where Indian uprisings against the Americans were believed to be supported by the British.

For some years, Presidents Thomas Jefferson and James Madison tried to prevent war between the United States and England. At the same time, many Americans (including Henry Clay and John Calhoun, two important congressmen) favored war because they wanted to teach England a lesson.

Finally, after several sea battles between British and American ships, the U.S. Congress declared war on England in June of 1812.

BACK TO BATTLE

In the months leading up to the declaration of war against England, Harrison's territory suffered from a new wave of Indian attacks. Between the Battle of Tippecanoe and the outbreak of the War of 1812, 20 whites were scalped in what is now the state of Indiana. A whole family was killed just five miles from Vincennes, the territorial capital. Many settlers abandoned their homesteads and moved into forts, and dozens of new forts had to be built. One of these, called "Fort Petticoat," had a garrison of rifle-carrying women.

In August of 1812, two months after the start of the war against England, Governor Harrison was given a commission by the U.S. War Department. He was made a major general of the Kentucky militia. Then, only a month later, he was promoted to the rank of brigadier general in the U.S. Army. Not long after that, in March of 1813, he was made major general in command of the whole Northwest Division of the U.S. Army. The War Department knew that Harrison's years of experience as an Indian fighter would be extremely valuable in this new war.

At Fort Meigs

Early in the War of 1812, the Americans suffered a serious defeat when General William Hull surrendered Fort Detroit—located where the city of Detroit, Michigan, now stands—to British forces who had marched down from Canada. Harrison was under orders to recapture Fort Detroit for the Americans.

While on their way to Fort Detroit, Harrison and his men stopped to rebuild Fort Meigs, on the Maumee River south of Fort Detroit. Fort Meigs had been weakened by Indian attacks. In the spring and early summer of 1813, while still at Fort Meigs, Harrison and his men were besieged by a mixed force of British soldiers and Indian warriors. On two occasions, the British and Indians surrounded the fort, attacked steadily for days at a time, and kept all food and supplies from reaching the men inside. Harrison and his men survived both sieges, however, forcing the disappointed attackers to fade into the forest without capturing the fort.

On at least one occasion, Tecumseh was among the besiegers at Fort Meigs. He sent Harrison a message that read:

> I have with me 800 braves. You have an equal number in your hiding place. Come out with them and give me battle. You talked like a brave when we met at Vincennes, and I respected you, but now you hide behind logs and the earth, like a ground hog. Give me your answer.

Harrison made no answer, and Tecumseh eventually withdrew. But he then attacked a column of soldiers coming up from Kentucky to relieve the siege of Fort Meigs and killed nearly 500 of them.

Standing Firm

Later in the summer, Harrison led his men eastward, to what is now called Sandusky Bay, across Lake Erie from Detroit. There they would wait while British and American ships battled to see who would control the lake.

The wait was tiresome to some of Harrison's men, many of whom were volunteers from Kentucky, not regular soldiers.

As the weeks wore on and no marching orders were given, the men began to speak—in whispers at first, but then more boldly—of deserting and going home to tend to their farms.

Hearing of this, Harrison called an assembly of all the men early one morning and made a solemn and patriotic speech. He told them that any men who were afraid or discouraged could leave with his permission, but no one stirred. When he stopped speaking, one shamefaced Kentucky colonel led the men in three cheers for "the hero of Tippecanoe." Harrison had put a stop to the threat of desertion.

Grand news arrived just a few days later. The U.S. Navy, under Captain Oliver Hazard Perry, had won a tremendous victory on Lake Erie. In one of the most important battles of the war, Perry had destroyed a squadron of British warships. The lake was now safe for Americans. Immediately, Harrison ordered his men to prepare for battle. They would cross the lake by boat and attack the British at Fort Detroit.

BATTLE OF THE THAMES

However, the British and their Indian allies did not wait idly at Fort Detroit to be captured or killed. They began a hasty retreat across Ontario, Canada. When Harrison arrived at Fort Detroit, he easily recaptured it. And then—not content with this victory—he set off in pursuit of the fleeing British and Indians.

There were 600 or so British soldiers, led by General Henry Proctor, and about 1,000 Indians, led by Tecumseh. The route they took through Ontario followed the course of a small river called the Thames, after the famous river of that name in London, England.

Harrison had a much larger force—about 2,100 Kentucky militiamen, 200 Indians who fought on the side of the Ameri-

Captain Oliver Hazard Perry's stunning victory over British naval forces on Lake Erie turned the tide of the War of 1812 in the Northwest. It also allowed Harrison to recapture Fort Detroit. (Library of Congress.)

cans, and 120 or so other volunteers. Harrison's army caught up with the enemy at a small settlement called Moravian Town, near Chatham, Ontario. There, on October 15, 1813, the Americans defeated the British and Indians in a desperate conflict that is known as the Battle of the Thames.

Proctor, the British general, ran from the American attack. He managed to escape in a carriage and made his way to safety. However, the shame of having deserted his men on the battlefield haunted Proctor for the rest of his life.

The Death of Tecumseh

Tecumseh, on the other hand, met a nobler end. He was shot during the Battle of the Thames, perhaps more than once. Nevertheless, he continued to stagger forward at the head of his men, shouting to them to remain firm and not give way. Then, just before darkness fell, both the whites and the Indians realized that Tecumseh's unmistakable voice had become silent. With the approach of night, the surviving Indians retreated into a nearby swamp and the victorious Americans set up camp.

As soon as dawn broke, Harrison and some of his men went to the battlefield to search for Tecumseh's body. Although Harrison ordered every man who had ever seen the Shawnee chief to examine all the fallen Indians, Tecumseh's corpse was not found. For some time afterward, Harrison could not believe that his enemy of so many years was really dead.

Many legends sprang up about what really happened to Tecumseh at the Thames. Some American soldiers gained fame by claiming to have killed him; some Indians claimed that he had survived the battle and would return some day to lead them to victory against the whites.

Gradually, over the years, the truth emerged, told by Indians who had been there. During the night after the battle, a band of loyal followers crept onto the battlefield, found Tecumseh's body, and secretly carried it away. They buried it in some unknown spot four or five miles from the battlefield. Many Indian graves have been found near Chatham, but none has been proven to be Tecumseh's. It is most likely that the final resting place of this courageous and determined Native American leader will forever remain a mystery.

An Even Greater Hero

The Battle of the Thames was one of the greatest American victories of the War of 1812. It secured the Northwest Territory for the United States in two ways: by driving the British back into Canada, and by causing the alliance between the Indians and the British to break up for good. Harrison's army took more than 600 prisoners and recaptured some cannons that the British had seized from the Americans during the Revolutionary War.

Perhaps most important to the United States was the fact that, with Tecumseh's death, the possibility of a confederacy of Indian tribes in the Northwest Territory was finally dead, too. William Henry Harrison was more than ever a hero after the Battle of the Thames.

RETURN TO NORTH BEND

The War of 1812 ended in 1814. That same year, Harrison resigned his army commission, retiring with the rank of major general. The government put him in charge of making treaties with the Indians after the war—a task for which he had plenty of experience.

The Fate of the Prophet

Tecumseh's brother, Tenskwautawa, the Shawnee Prophet, was for a while nearly as powerful and as important among the Indians of the Northwest Territory as was Tecumseh himself. His religious teachings spread far and wide, and Indians of many tribes flocked to his side.

After Harrison defeated the Indians at Tippecanoe, however, many of the Prophet's followers lost faith in him. In the eyes of many, he had shown himself to be a very poor leader. Tecumseh was especially furious at the Prophet and refused to have anything to do with him for several months.

The outcast Prophet wandered through much of the Northwest Territory after the Battle of Tippecanoe. He continued to preach, but few took him seriously. He did see Tecumseh at least once before the great war leader died. After the British captured Fort Detroit, Tecumseh spent some time there with his new allies. He was hopeful that the Indians and the British would together defeat the Americans, and in this mood of optimism and good spirits he permitted Tenskwautawa to visit him. They shared a pipe—an Indian ritual that meant "peace"—then the Prophet wandered westward again and Tecumseh met his fate on the banks of the Thames River.

After the War of 1812, most of the Indians of the Northwest Territory were forced by the U.S. government to move to new lands beyond the Mississippi River. In recognition of the services of Tecumseh in the war, however, the British government gave the Prophet a small pension that provided him with money to live on for the rest of his life.

Tenskwautawa wound up in Kansas. There, it is said, he took to drinking again and grew fat and lazy. He remained an impressive character, however. The painter George Catlin spent the years 1829–1837 roaming the territories west of the Mississippi. He knew the Prophet and described him this way: "There is no doubt that he has been a very shrewd and influential man, but circumstances have destroyed him." Catlin painted a portrait of the Prophet that gives his strong, dominating features a look of dignity and pride. The Shawnee Prophet died in Wyandotte County, Kansas, in 1837.

With the war behind him, Harrison had no desire to become governor of the Indiana Territory again. He was now 41 years old and had been in Indiana for nearly 15 years. His father-in-law, Judge Symmes, had died, leaving a large amount of money and property that was involved in complicated wills and settlements. Harrison felt that he was needed to help sort out this business, and he was ready to try private life for a change. So he and Anna took their large family back to North Bend, Ohio, where Harrison owned a large farm.

The Harrisons settled into a comfortable home there. Harrison became involved in local affairs. He was an official of the Christ Episcopal Church in Cincinnati and a trustee of Cincinnati College.

POLITICAL LIFE

After so many years of public life, Harrison was not content to remain a private citizen for long. In 1816, at the suggestion of friends, he ran for a seat in the U.S. House of Representatives, where he had once served as the delegate of the Northwest Territory. This time he hoped to represent the Cincinnati district. He won the seat after defeating four candidates and went off to Washington, D.C. Anna remained in Ohio with the children.

Congressman Harrison

Harrison's term as a representative was not particularly noteworthy. He served as chairman of the House Committee on the Militia. His strong belief in the importance of a powerful fighting force led him to recommend that *all* males should receive military training. He also spoke up in favor of the government making payments to widows of soldiers and to war veterans.

In the debate over slavery that was beginning to divide the United States, Harrison tended to side with the slaveowners of the South, perhaps because of his Virginia background. he believed that there should be no limits on the spread of slavery into new territories, just as he had believed when he was governor of the Indiana Territory.

After one term in the House of Representatives, from 1816 to 1819, Harrison decided not to try for re-election. He hoped that the President would appoint him as minister (an office similar to that of a present-day ambassador) to Russia. The post was considered quite an honor, but Harrison failed to win it.

Senator Harrison

When Harrison returned to Cincinnati, some of his supporters named him as a candidate for the Ohio state senate. He was elected a state senator in 1819 and served one term, until 1821. When he ran for re-election to this post, he lost by 500 votes.

During the next three years, Harrison tried and failed to win several political offices: the governorship of Ohio, his old seat in the House of Representatives, and a seat in the U.S. Senate. Finally, in 1825, he was elected to the U.S. Senate, where he served until 1828. He was chairman of the Senate Committee on Militia and the Military. In this role, he urged the government to raise the pay of soldiers in the army and to add more ships and men to the navy.

A FOREIGN DIPLOMAT

During his term in the U.S. Senate, Harrison loyally supported President John Quincy Adams. He voted for many of the bills that Adams favored. The President (the son of former President John Adams) did not have a very high opinion of Harrison's mental powers. Adams said of Harrison that he had "a lively and active, but shallow, mind." Nevertheless, he rewarded Harrison's loyalty by appointing him to a ministerial post in 1828.

The posting was not to Russia or to one of the European capitals, which Harrison might have preferred. Instead, Adams asked Harrison to represent the United States in Colombia, a new country that had been formed out of the Spanish colonies in South America. Harrison accepted the position without much enthusiasm, partly because of the good salary that came with it.

Simon Bolivar is often called "the liberator of South America" because he led the Spanish colonies in their fight for independence. Harrison's brief adventure in foreign diplomacy took him to Colombia, where he met Bolivar. (Library of Congress.)

Harrison arrived in Bogota, the capital of Colombia, in February of 1829. Just one month later, however, events back home in the United States ended his career as a foreign diplomat. Andrew Jackson, who had been elected President in the fall of 1828, took office in March of 1829. He was a Democrat, the first President to be elected as a member of the present-day Democratic Party. Adams, on the other hand, was a member of what came to be called the Whig Party, the ancestor of today's Republican Party.

Appointment Withdrawn

When one political party takes control of the presidency from another, it often happens that the people appointed by the previous President are removed from office by his successor. So it was with Harrison. Jackson did not want any Whigs in diplomatic posts while he was President, so he sent word to Harrison in Bogota that his appointment had been withdrawn.

However, because Harrison's replacement did not arrive in Bogota until September of 1829, he continued to carry out his duties until that time. Harrison then left Colombia for the United States and arrived home in February of 1830, bringing a bright blue and scarlet parrot as a souvenir of South America.

During his brief term as a diplomat, Harrison actually did very little. He made the acquaintance of General Simon Bolivar, the South American patriot who had led that continent's wars of liberation against the Spanish and then headed Colombia's government. In a letter to Bolivar, Harrison rather pompously advised the general that "the stongest of all governments is that which is most free."

Many Colombians resented Harrison's letter, because it seemed to them to be a criticism of their own government and because they did not care to be lectured to on democracy by the United States. The letter was widely quoted at home, however, and gave Harrison a reputation as a statesman that he did not quite deserve.

Money Troubles

Although he was eager to continue his career in public office, Harrison found few opportunities to do so during Andrew Jackson's eight years in the White House. Jackson, who was another hero of the War of 1812, despised the Whigs. He especially disliked Harrison because Harrison had criticized Jackson's handling of the war against the Seminole Indians in Florida.

So Harrison retired once again to the farm in North Bend. He and Anna presided over their family, which had changed considerably. Several of their children were now married and starting families of their own; Lucy had died in 1826 and John died in 1830.

The Harrisons also experienced money troubles in the 1830s. The farm was not earning enough to pay the family's expenses. In 1834, Harrison accepted the humble position of court clerk in Hamilton County in order to receive a modest salary. At this low point in his career, far from the victories of the battlefield and equally far from the seats of power in the nation's capital, Harrison may have wondered bitterly whether his days of glory were over. He did not suspect that his greatest glory was yet to come.

Chapter 9

President Harrison

As President Jackson's second term in the White House drew to a close, the nation's Whigs began planning a campaign to elect a Whig President. They knew that Martin Van Buren, Jackson's Vice-President and friend, would probably be the Democrats' candidate for President. They looked around for a someone who might get enough votes to beat Van Buren.

The Whig Party was a very young political organization, formed only a few years before out of the remains of several previous parties. There were a number of prominent men among the Whigs, including Henry Clay of Kentucky, but some party leaders felt that Clay was too controversial. For years he had been a statesman and speech-maker in the halls of Congress. He was a man of very definite opinions who never hesitated to say what he thought. Many Americans admired him, but many others distrusted or disliked him. Daniel Webster of Massachusetts was another possibility, but to some people he represented the well-to-do, well-educated East Coast upper class.

SEEKING A CANDIDATE

The Whig leaders decided that they needed a candidate with more widespread appeal – someone who was not well known just for having a lot of opinions. If the candidate happened to be a war hero, so much the better. And now that Indiana and Illinois had become states, a candidate who was popular in the region that was once the Northwest Territory might get support from voters there.

Recognizing that the Whigs needed a candidate, Harrison was very eager to fill that need. He made speaking tours through Indiana and Illinois, promoting himself as a presidential candidate. Many towns staged anniversary celebrations of his victories at Tippecanoe and the Thames. Newspapers ran editorials praising "Old Tip's" patriotism and devotion to duty.

When it was suggested to him that he might be a good running mate for Webster, Harrison replied indignantly that he would not consider running for Vice-President "on that ticket or any other." After years of obscurity, he sensed an opportunity to become President, and he would not settle for second place.

FIRST CAMPAIGN

Harrison gained so many supporters among the Whigs that when the party met in 1836 to select a presidential candidate, he was nominated. Because Harrison, clerk of the Hamilton County, Ohio, court of common pleas, had never played a very significant role in national politics, his views and abilities were unknown to most Americans. They knew of him only as the hero of Tippecanoe and the Thames. And because the leaders of the Whig Party wanted to keep it that way, they warned Harrison not to say anything definite on any subject.

A Close-Mouthed Approach

A leading Whig, banker Nicholas Biddle of Philadelphia, went so far as to give party heads this advice about Harrison:

> Let him say not one single word about his principles, or his creed—let him say nothing—promise nothing. Let no Committee or Convention—no town meeting ever extract from him a single word about what he thinks now, or what he will do hereafter. Let the use of pen and ink be forbidden as if he were a mad poet.

In keeping with this close-mouthed approach, Harrison made few speeches or public appearances during the campaign. Perhaps his silence was a mistake—or perhaps the American voters were largely satisfied with the way Democratic President Jackson had been running the country for eight years. When they went to the polls on November 8, 1836, they elected another Democrat, Martin Van Buren. Harrison returned to his farm and his job as court clerk.

THE ELECTION OF 1840

Four years later, the Whigs again found themselves looking toward North Bend. Once again, Henry Clay expected to receive his party's presidential nomination, and once again the Whig leaders decided that he was not likely to win the election. One thing that worked against Clay was that he held a high position in the Masons, a semi-secret men's society. Many Whigs were strongly opposed to the Masons, who were wrongly believed to be dangerously anti-American. These Whigs blocked Clay's attempts to secure the nomination.

Tippecanoe and Tyler, Too

When the Whigs met at Harrisburg, Pennsylvania, in December of 1839 to choose a candidate, Harrison received 148 votes to Clay's 90. Clay was waiting in Washington to hear the results of the convention. When he learned that Harrison had again been chosen over him, he leaped to his feet and cried, "My friends are not worth the powder and shot it would take to kill them!"

However, Clay's friend and supporter, John Tyler of Virginia, was selected as the Whig candidate for Vice-President. Because Tyler had hoped to be Clay's running mate, the relationship between Harrison and Tyler was never warm. The choice of these two men, however, produced a catchy campaign slogan: "Tippecanoe and Tyler, Too."

Scorn and Criticism

The news that Harrison would be running for President in 1840 caused a variety of reaction. Thomas Hart Benton, a Democratic U.S. senator from Missouri, remarked that "availability was the only ability sought by the Whigs," suggesting that Harrison's sole qualification to be President was that he was willing to run for the office.

The *Baltimore American*, a Democratic newspaper, published an article that was supposed to be highly critical of Harrison. Said the writer scornfully, "Give him a barrel of hard cider and settle a pension of $2,000 a year on him and, my word for it, he will sit the remainder of his days in a log cabin by the side of a sea coal fire and study moral philosophy." The writer meant by this that Harrison was a man of little ambition who would cut an unimpressive figure as President.

To Harrison's dismay, however, the Whigs were delighted

The Log Cabin Campaign of 1840 was filled with gimmicks of all sorts. Harrison's supporters rallied to the image of the log cabin, which represented simple all-American values. Here the flag bears the motto "Harrison & Tyler" and the barrels next to the cabin are labeled "Hard Cider." Harrison, on the left, is seen greeting a wounded solider. (Library of Congress.)

with this image of their candidate. They seized upon it with glee and immediately organized one of the first modern-style presidential campaigns, complete with songs, buttons, and colorful gimmicks of all sorts to stir up public interest.

The Log Cabin Campaign

Almost overnight, William Henry Harrison was transformed into the "Log Cabin Candidate." He was presented to the voters as a typical frontiersman, full of simple all-American virtues. Although he was a well-educated Virginian from an aristocratic family who lived in a 22-room mansion in North Bend, Ohio, his campaign managers wanted voters to think of him as a symbol of the common man. Van Buren, on the other hand, was portrayed as a rich, sophisticated snob with expensive habits–even though this image was no more true than the "log cabin" image of Harrison.

Harrison's supporters built log cabins as meeting-places in hundreds of towns. Parades, rallies, and conventions of all sorts were held. Barrel after barrel of cider was served out to voters across the land. A liquor manufacturer in Philadelphia introduced a new product called Old Cabin Whiskey.

Whig newsletters were produced with names like "The Hard Cider Press," "Old Tip's Broom," and "The Log Cabin." Tippecanoe Tobacco and Tippecanoe Shaving Soap went on sale in stores. Popular new dances included the Harrison Hoedown and the Tippecanoe Quick-Step. And the log cabin symbol appeared on scores of souvenirs, including handkerchiefs, teacups, sunbonnets, and plates. As a publicity stunt, some of Harrison's supporters rolled a large ball all the way from Kentucky to Baltimore, singing:

> What has caused this great commotion, motion,
> Our country through?
> It's the ball a-rolling on
> For Tippecanoe and Tyler, too
> And with them we'll beat the little Van, Van, Van,
> Van is a used up man.

Acres of Crowds

Amid all this wild excitement, Harrison traveled from town to town making speeches. He avoided difficult issues, such as slavery, and simply talked in general terms about the greatness of America. Some of his speeches were three hours long.

As it was rolled through town after town by the Whigs, this giant ball gained much attention for Harrison's presidential campaign. A similar campaign ball stunt was later used by Harrison's grandson, Benjamin Harrison. (Library of Congress.)

The crowds that came to hear Harrison were so large that they could be measured in acres. Before or after his speeches, he often led parades, riding on a large wagon upon which a log cabin had been built. There were cider barrels in front of the cabin and live raccoons frisking about on the roof.

The Votes Are Cast

The thrills and gimmicks of the Log Cabin Campaign certainly helped Harrison win the presidential election of 1840. But the Democrats were also hurt by the severe money problems the nation had experienced in 1837, when an economic depression hit. Many banks had to close, and many people lost their savings. Goods such as sugar, tea, and cloth became more expensive. People blamed the Democrats for the "Panic of 1837," as this crisis was called. Americans were ready for a change of government.

More people voted in the election of 1840 than in any previous presidential election. Nearly 2½ million men cast their votes in November—an increase of 50 percent over the number who had voted just four years before.

The voting in the electoral college ran strongly in Harrison's favor. He received 234 votes to Van Buren's 19. In the popular vote, though—that is, the votes cast by individual citizens—the results were much closer. Harrison received only 150,000 more votes than Van Buren. Either way, however, William Henry Harrison was elected ninth President of the United States.

An Old President

Harrison was thrilled with his long-awaited victory, and he did not try to hide it. Van Buren complained, "He is as tickled with the Presidency as a young woman with a new bonnet." Even Anna, Harrison's loyal wife of many years, had a complaint of her own. She said, "I wish that my husband's friends had left him where he is, happy and contented in retirement."

Harrison was 67 years old when he was elected President, making him the oldest American President before Ronald Reagan in the 1980s. His wife may have worried that the strain of the presidency would be bad for his health. Because she herself fell ill just before they were due to leave for Harrison's inauguration in Washington, she was unable to accompany him.

HARRISON IN WASHINGTON

The nation's capital threw a grand party for Harrison when he arrived to take office. Dozens of dances, parties, and dinners were held in his honor. One event took place in a huge hall built to look like a giant log cabin and lit by 1,800 candles.

Inauguration day, March 4, 1841, was cold and blustery. But large crowds lined the streets to see the parade and watch the new President being sworn into office. The crowd cheered for 10 minutes when Harrison rose to speak. Before long, however, many in the crowd were shivering with the chill and wondering when he would sit down again.

A Long Speech

Harrison's inauguration speech was the longest in American history—nearly two hours. Daniel Webster, a noted speechmaker, had offered to write the speech for Harrison, but Harrison insisted on doing it himself. Webster later said peevishly that "Old Tip took a very long time to say very little."

The speech did not say much about specific issues facing the nation but was full of stirring references to patriotism

Crowds thronged Washington, D.C., on March 4, 1841, to hear "Old Tip" sworn in as President. His two-hour inauguration speech was the longest in American history. (Library of Congress.)

and military glory. In spite of the cold, Harrison delivered the speech without a hat, gloves, or an overcoat. Midway through, it began to rain. He continued without a break.

Finally the speech was over and the crowd dispersed. Accompanied by his son William Henry, Jr., and his daughter-in-law Jane, who was to serve as his official hostess until Anna could arrive from North Bend, Harrison led the parade to the White House. That evening he attended three formal balls. When the long day was over, he was exhausted and chilled. Before long, it was clear that he had caught a bad cold.

Selecting a Cabinet

Like all new Presidents, Harrison had to appoint a Cabinet—the group of advisors who would head the major branches of the government. And like all Presidents, he awarded Cabinet posts to people who had helped him or were members of his own party.

Daniel Webster, one of the leading Whigs, received the highest Cabinet post, secretary of state. He recommended his friend, Thomas Ewing of Ohio, as secretary of the treasury, and Harrison made the appointment. John Bell of Tennessee was made secretary of war; John Crittenden of Kentucky, attorney general; George Badger of North Carolina, secretary of the navy; and Francis Granger of New York—who had been the Whig candidate for Vice-President in 1836—was made postmaster general.

The task of selecting a Cabinet was difficult for Harrison because so many people asked him for Cabinet posts. People wrote and visited to request other jobs, too. In fact, at times the new President was nearly besieged with people seeking appointments to government offices.

A Short Term in Office

Getting his Cabinet appointed was just about the only thing Harrison was able to accomplish as President. Although he had hoped to have a long and productive presidency, his cold became worse and turned into pneumonia. He took to his bed on March 28.

By April 3, it was clear that Harrison's condition was

One month after his triumphant inauguration, Harrison died in the White House of pneumonia. He was the first President to die in office. (Library of Congress.)

serious. "I am ill, very ill, much more so than they think me," he murmured at one point. Not long afterward, he fell into unconsciousness, from which he never recovered.

Harrison's words might have been directed at John Tyler, his Vice-President. They were, "I wish you to understand the true principles of the government. I wish them carried out. I ask nothing more." He died just after midnight on April 4, one month after being inaugurated.

Death of a President

William Henry Harrison was the first American President to die in office. An Episcopal funeral service was held in the East Room of the White House, and then the President's body was carried to the Capitol building, where it lay in state as mourners passed by. Harrison was buried in Washington, but in June the coffin was moved to a cemetery in North Bend.

It is interesting to note that Vice-President Tyler had some difficulty in establishing himself as President after Harrison's death. As this was the first time a President had died in office, not everyone was sure of how to proceed. Some people felt that Tyler was only a sort of "acting President" who should take orders from the Cabinet or Congress because he had not been elected to the nation's top office. But Tyler, although he was not a particularly impressive President, was a man of firm character. At his first Cabinet meeting, he let Harrison's advisors know that *he* would make the decisions in the White House. Nearly all of the Cabinet members resigned in annoyance.

The Family Carries On

Harrison's wife, Anna, never was able to join her husband for the short time he was President. Because of her illness, she had not arrived in Washington at the time of his death.

Benjamin Harrison, the grandson of William Henry Harrison, fought for the Union in the Civil War and was President from 1889 to 1893. (Library of Congress.)

Anna Symmes Harrison received the first pension to be granted a President's widow; it was in the amount of $25,000. She outlived most of her children and continued to live in North Bend until 1855, when the home was destroyed by fire. After that, she resided with John Scott Harrison, her only surviving son.

Anna died in 1864 and was buried next to President Harrison in North Bend. Some years later, John Scott Harrison's son Benjamin was elected 23rd President of the United States. William Henry Harrison is the only President whose grandson has also held that office.

Harrison is not remembered as a great President—nor as a bad one. But he is remembered for military leadership and heroism that helped write the history of the American frontier.

Bibliography

Cleaves, Freeman. *Old Tippecanoe: William Henry Harrison and His Times*. New York: Scribner's, 1939. One of the few full-length accounts of Harrison's life and career, this book was reprinted in 1969.

Edmunds, R. David. *Tecumseh and the Quest for Indian Leadership*. Boston: Little, Brown, 1984. A leading scholar of Shawnee history describes Tecumseh's struggle to unite the Indians of the Northwest Territory. The book includes discussions of Tecumseh's battles with Harrison.

Peckham, Howard Henry. *Young Tippecanoe*. Indianapolis: Bobbs-Merrill, 1957. The emphasis in this book is on Harrison's family, childhood, and early career as an Indian fighter. The book is aimed at young readers and is illustrated.

Tucker, Glenn. *Tecumseh: Vision of Glory*. Indianapolis: Bobbs-Merrill, 1956. This is one of the most readable and colorful accounts of Tecumseh's life. It also contains much information about the Prophet and about Harrison. The author is clearly sympathetic to the Indian cause but presents the facts fairly and evenhandedly.

Young, Stanley. *Tippecanoe and Tyler, Too*! New York: Random House, 1957. Written for young readers, this book focuses on Harrison's early years and the Battle of Tippecanoe. His later political life is described briefly, without much detail.

Index

PRESIDENTS OF THE UNITED STATES

GEORGE WASHINGTON	L. Falkof	0-944483-19-4
JOHN ADAMS	R. Stefoff	0-944483-10-0
THOMAS JEFFERSON	R. Stefoff	0-944483-07-0
JAMES MADISON	B. Polikoff	0-944483-22-4
JAMES MONROE	R. Stefoff	0-944483-11-9
JOHN QUINCY ADAMS	M. Greenblatt	0-944483-21-6
ANDREW JACKSON	R. Stefoff	0-944483-08-9
MARTIN VAN BUREN	R. Ellis	0-944483-12-7
WILLIAM HENRY HARRISON	R. Stefoff	0-944483-54-2
JOHN TYLER	L. Falkof	0-944483-60-7
JAMES K. POLK	M. Greenblatt	0-944483-04-6
ZACHARY TAYLOR	D. Collins	0-944483-17-8
MILLARD FILLMORE	K. Law	0-944483-61-5
FRANKLIN PIERCE	F. Brown	0-944483-25-9
JAMES BUCHANAN	D. Collins	0-944483-62-3
ABRAHAM LINCOLN	R. Stefoff	0-944483-14-3
ANDREW JOHNSON	R. Stevens	0-944483-16-X
ULYSSES S. GRANT	L. Falkof	0-944483-02-X
RUTHERFORD B. HAYES	N. Robbins	0-944483-23-2
JAMES A. GARFIELD	F. Brown	0-944483-63-1
CHESTER A. ARTHUR	R. Stevens	0-944483-05-4
GROVER CLEVELAND	D. Collins	0-944483-01-1
BENJAMIN HARRISON	R. Stevens	0-944483-15-1
WILLIAM McKINLEY	D. Collins	0-944483-55-0
THEODORE ROOSEVELT	R. Stefoff	0-944483-09-7
WILLIAM H. TAFT	L. Falkof	0-944483-56-9
WOODROW WILSON	D. Collins	0-944483-18-6
WARREN G. HARDING	A. Canadeo	0-944483-64-X
CALVIN COOLIDGE	R. Stevens	0-944483-57-7

HERBERT C. HOOVER	B. Polikoff	0-944483-58-5
FRANKLIN D. ROOSEVELT	M. Greenblatt	0-944483-06-2
HARRY S. TRUMAN	D. Collins	0-944483-00-3
DWIGHT D. EISENHOWER	R. Ellis	0-944483-13-5
JOHN F. KENNEDY	L. Falkof	0-944483-03-8
LYNDON B. JOHNSON	L. Falkof	0-944483-20-8
RICHARD M. NIXON	R. Stefoff	0-944483-59-3
GERALD R. FORD	D. Collins	0-944483-65-8
JAMES E. CARTER	D. Richman	0-944483-24-0
RONALD W. REAGAN	N. Robbins	0-944483-66-6
GEORGE H.W. BUSH	R. Stefoff	1-56074-033-7
WILLIAM J. CLINTON	D. Collins	1-56074-056-6

GARRETT EDUCATIONAL CORPORATION
130 EAST 13TH STREET
ADA, OK 74820